MAKERS
of the
MUSLIM
WORLD

Ibn Hamdis the Sicilian

TITLES IN THE MAKERS OF THE MUSLIM WORLD SERIES

Series Editors: Professor Khaled El-Rouayheb, Harvard University, and Professor Sabine Schmidtke, Institute for Advanced Study, Princeton

'Abd al-Ghani al-Nabulusi, Samer Akkach
'Abd al-Malik, Chase F. Robinson
Abd al-Rahman al-Kawakibi, Itzchak Weismann
'Abd al-Rahman III, Maribel Fierro
'Abd al-Rahman b. 'Amr al-Awza'i, Steven C. Judd
Abu Nuwas, Philip F. Kennedy
Ahmad al-Mansur, Mercedes García-Arenal
Ahmad ibn Hanbal, Christopher Melchert
Ahmad ibn Tulun, Matthew S. Gordon
Ahmad Riza Khan Barelwi, Usha Sanyal
Aisha al-Ba'uniyya, Th. Emil Homerin
Akbar, André Wink
Al Ma'mun, Michael Cooperson
Al-Mutanabbi, Margaret Larkin
Amir Khusraw, Sunil Sharma
Ashraf 'Ali Thanawi, Muhammad Qasim Zaman
Beshir Agha, Jane Hathaway
Chinggis Khan, Michal Biran
Elijah Muhammad, Herbert Berg
Fazlallah Astarabadi and the Hurufis, Shahzad Bashir
Ghazali, Eric Ormsby
Hasan al-Banna, Gudrun Krämer
Husain Ahmad Madani, Barbara D. Metcalf
Ibn 'Abd al-Wahhab, Michael Crawford
Ibn 'Arabi, William C. Chittick
Ibn Taymiyya, Jon Hoover
Ibn Tufayl, Taneli Kukkonen
Ikhwan al-Safa', Godefroid de Callataÿ
Imam Shafi'i, Kecia Ali
Karim Khan Zand, John R. Perry
Mehmed Ali, Khaled Fahmy
Mu'awiya ibn Abi Sufyan, R. Stephen Humphreys
Muhammad Abduh, Mark Sedgwick
Mulla Sadra, Sayeh Meisami
Nasser, Joel Gordon
Nazira Zeineddine, Miriam Cooke
Sa'di, Homa Katouzian
Shah 'Abbas, Sholeh A. Quinn
Shaykh Mufid, Tamima Bayhom-Daou
Usama ibn Munqidh, Paul M. Cobb
'Uthman ibn 'Affan, Heather N. Keaney

For current information and details of other books in the series, please visit oneworld-publications.com/makers-of-the-muslim-world

MAKERS
of the
MUSLIM
WORLD

Ibn Hamdis the Sicilian

Eulogist for a Falling Homeland

WILLIAM GRANARA

ONEWORLD
ACADEMIC

Oneworld Academic

An imprint of Oneworld Publications

Published by Oneworld Academic in 2021

A CIP record for this title is available from the British Library

ISBN 978-1-78607-846-9
eISBN 978-1-78607-847-6

Map © Eric Edstam

Typeset by Geethik Technologies
Printed and bound in Great Britain by Clays Ltd, Elcograf S.p.A.

Oneworld Publications
10 Bloomsbury Street
London WC1B 3SR
England

CONTENTS

Notes to the Reader ix
Acknowledgements xi
Preface xiii
Map of Ibn Hamdis's World xv

1 BORN UNDER A BAD SIGN 1
The Kalbids of Sicily 2
Muslim Sicily Unraveling 3
Born in Syracuse, Becoming a Poet 6
Education in an Early Jihadi Frontier 8
The Rise of an Indigenous Muslim-Sicilian Culture 11
Poetry in Muslim Sicily, From Philology to Art and Politics 12
Crafting a Poetics of 'Homeland' 14

2 DILEMMA: TO REMAIN OR DEPART 19
Sojourn in Sfax: Maintaining the Ifriqiya-Sicily Connection 19
Asad ibn al-Furat: Muslim Sicily's Founding Father 21
Ibn Hawqal's Sicilian Chapter 24
In the Shadow of the Norman Conquest 26

3 THE FIRST DESERT CROSSING 33
Ifriqiya: A Divided and Turbulent Motherland 34
The Zirid Dynasty of Ifriqiya 35
The 'Arabs' of Eleventh-Century Ifriqiya 37
On the Desert Highway: Traveling with Arab Companions 40

4 *LA DOLCE VITA* IN SEVILLE 47
The 'Abbadid Kingdom of Seville 48
Muslim Spain and Muslim Sicily: A Comparative View 50
Elegy to a Father 54

Serving the Patron: The Political Panegyric 57
Court Poet as Court Functionary 60
The Looming Threat of the Christian Reconquest 61
Poetic Sparring: Poet as Client, Poet as Competitor 63

5 FROM THE DARK CLOUDS OF AL-ZALLAQA TO A SECOND EXILE 69
Confrontation at Badajoz: Enter the Almoravids 70
The Battle of al-Zallaqa 72
The Fall of the ʻAbbadids of Seville 80

6 1091: *ANNUS HORRIBILIS* AND THE SECOND DESERT CROSSING 85
Intermission at Qalʻat Bani Hammad 87
Return to Mahdia 94
Connecting to the Zirids: Praise and Blame for Tamim 95
Vigilant Eye on the Norman Conquest 100
Ode to a Falling Homeland 102
Back to the Family in Sfax: Mourning the Loss of an Aunt and a Wife 105

7 THE POETICS OF JIHAD: AT THE ZIRID COURT IN MAHDIA 111
At the Court of Yahya ibn Tamim 112
Revolt and Murder at the Zirid Palace 115
Breaking Ranks in Gabes 118
From Seville to Nicotera and Mahdia: The Almoravids Move East 119
Victory at al-Dimas 121
The Almohads on the Horizon 123

8 TIME OF REFLECTION: ASCETIC VERSES AND ARABS AT THE NORMAN COURT 125
Retreat into Devotional Verse 125
Arabs and Muslim Culture at the Norman Court in Palermo 129

9 TWILIGHT: BLINDNESS, LOSS, AND DEFEAT 135
Losing Sight 136
Sicily Forever on the Mind 138
Elegy to a Nephew and Family History 139
Mourning a Daughter, Mourning a Homeland 141
Death and Burial 144
Ibn Hamdis's Legacy in History and Literature 145

Bibliography 151
Index 153

NOTES TO THE READER

In transliterating Arabic names and terms, I follow the IJMES system minus macrons and diacritics, with the exception of the glottal stop (left-facing apostrophe) and the 'ayn (right-facing apostrophe).

With regard to geographical names I use modern usage, but I insert the Arabic transliteration followed in parentheses only when it first appears in the text: i.e., Sfax (*Safaqus*); Kairouan (*al-Qayrawan*).

I use *Ifriqiya*, *Maghreb*, and *North Africa* which overlap in meaning in many contexts: *Ifriqiya* refers to a geographical and political entity from the ninth through the thirteenth centuries; *Maghreb* is used to designate the linguistic, cultural, and geographical expanse of Arab-Berber North Africa, from southern Morocco to eastern Libya; *North Africa* refers to what is generally meant in the modern geopolitical lexicon.

My chronology of events in the life of Ibn Hamdis is based on historical references to contemporaneous people and events, the brief notations of poems provided by the presumed editor of the *Diwan*, and explicit comments by the poet throughout his verses. Since classical Arabic historiography is based on a lunar calendar (*Hijri*), which alternates between twenty-nine and thirty days per month, it provides dates that do not correspond directly with those in a solar calendar (*Gregorian*). In translating these dates, I use the dating system of the common era (AD, CE) familiar to my readership. In the process, there may appear to be miscalculations, such as discrepancies between a person's age in lunar years and solar years; but my goal is to remain as faithful as possible to the original Arabic sources.

Over the past two decades I have published a number of articles on Muslim Sicily, many of which deal specifically with Ibn Hamdis. It is only natural that I draw from them on numerous occasions. I refer the reader to my Bibliography at the end of the manuscript for a listing of these, and other, sources.

In translating Ibn Hamdis's poetry into English, I tend to remain literal, i.e., as faithful as possible to the original. I do not attempt to recreate meters or rhyming in the English, and I use an asterisk to indicate explanations of obscure language not easily understood in the literal translation. From time to time, I point out examples of punning that enhance the effect of the poem. The informed reader of classical Arabic poetry will detect numerous examples of Ibn Hamdis's references, borrowings, and other forms of intertextuality with works by the masters of Arabic poetry. Since my primary goal is to extract the autobiographical voice of the poet, I refrain from elaborating on these examples. Ibn Hamdis was a consummate wordsmith known for drawing upon archaic vocabulary, coining new meanings, and crafting unusual or innovative metaphors that at times obscure the intended meaning of the verse. Over the many years of my readings, consultations with highly informed colleagues, and extensive research on medieval Muslim Sicilian history, I have taken, at times, liberties with translation in consideration of the detail of Ibn Hamdis's life story. Any alternate or erroneous readings of verses are of my own making.

Finally, I rely on modern terminology to express concepts or meanings not in use during the eleventh and twelfth centuries but which nonetheless best express appropriate meanings. I recognize the anachronism therein, and I beg my readers' indulgence in this regard: i.e., '*secular humanism,*' '*pan-Arabism*,' Sicilian '*nationalism.*'

ACKNOWLEDGEMENTS

Writing this book has from time to time reminded me of the opening line of Emily Dickinson's "There is No Frigate Like a Book." It was a journey that crossed oceans and seas, stretching over a long period of time and many parts of the world. I first made the acquaintance of 'Abd al-Jabbar Ibn Hamdis during my graduate school days in Philadelphia in the late seventies as I worked my way through Michele Amari's *Biblioteca Arabo-Sicula*. In the summer of 1982, I had the good fortune of purchasing a copy of Ibn Hamdis's *Diwan* at the Halaby Book Shop in downtown Cairo. Following a day trip to Souse, Tunisia, in 1989, the place where Muslim Sicilian history began, I returned to my then home in Sidi Bou Said and, leafing through the *Diwan*, I was attracted especially to his short description (*wasf*) poems. Then in 1993, having joined the Department of Near Eastern Languages and Civilizations at Harvard, I developed a more serious interest in the *Diwan* not only for its artistic value but also as a rich source for the study of Muslim Sicilian history. My first public lecture was delivered at Harvard's Humanities Center (now named the Mahindra Center for the Humanities), which was later published by *Edebyat* (1998) through the encouragement and meticulous editing of my late friend and colleague, Wolfhart P. Heinrichs.

In January 2004, I began a semester of sabbatical leave in Rome, shuttling between the Vatican Library and PISAI (Pontifical Institute for Arabic and Islamic Studies) in Trastevere. I remember how excited I was to finally be able to hold and leaf through one of the two extant manuscripts of the *Diwan*—the other being in St. Petersburg—after months during which the Vatican's Arabic-Islamic collection was closed for cleaning. My months in Rome were dedicated to working through Ibn Hamdis's poetry, and culminated in a lecture I delivered at the Oriental Institute at Oxford (during an Alitalia strike, no less!) at the kind invitation of my former Arabic student and now noted historian of Islam, Chase Robinson. Since that time, I have had the good fortune of numerous opportunities to present my work on Ibn Hamdis in Beirut, Tunis, Palermo, Toronto, Montreal, Washington D.C., Santa Cruz, and Los Angeles.

In the long journey to complete this book, I have many people to thank:

Above all I thank Alex Metcalfe and Brian Catlos, extraordinary historians of the medieval Mediterranean, for their vast knowledge, wisdom, and generosity in reading and critiquing my work; also, to Sinan Antoon, Khaled al-Masri, and Shady Nasser for their impeccable philology, linguistic skills, and poetic sensibilities in helping me read difficult passages and offering superb suggestions for translation. In writing this book I benefitted from scholars, students, and friends whose work in the medieval Mediterranean world enriched my own: the late Maria Rosa Menocal, Karla Mallette, Jeremy Johns, Francesca Corrao, Robert Wisnovsky, Nicola Carpentieri, Eric Calderwood, and Ali Asgar Alibhai. I thank Eric Edstam of Harvard's CMES who designed the map, *Ibn Hamdis's World*, and who has been my editorial and technology right hand throughout this journey.

To Khaled El-Rouayheb, I express my thanks for his interest in publishing this book, and to my editor, Jonathan Bentley-Smith, a standing ovation for his guidance, patience, and professionalism.

PREFACE

'Abd al-Jabbar Ibn Hamdis was born in 1055 in the city of Syracuse, located in the province of Val di Noto, on the island of Sicily and died in 1133, in a locale which remains a matter of historical speculation. At the time of his birth Sicily was reaping the benefits of a century of cultural development after a long period of conquest. As a child he was provided with a traditional Arabo-Islamic education which at that time consisted of the multiple branches of Quranic studies, Arabic grammar and philology, and classical Arabic poetry to which he would dedicate his entire long life of eighty years.

The island of Sicily at that time was also witnessing internal divisions that wreaked havoc on the political unity and social cohesion of the Muslim community. The carving up of the island among local warlords resulted in an easy entrance for the Norman armies which had come by this time to conquer much of the Italian mainland. The capture of the city of Palermo in 1072 under the command of Count Roger I was a watershed moment in the history of medieval Sicily. Six years later, Ibn Hamdis, at the age of twenty-four, packed up his family and bags, and followed the path of many Muslims who had been emigrating from the island since the disintegration of the last Muslim ruling dynasty, the Kalbids, some thirty years prior.

The first stop on his long road in exile was in the city of Sfax located on the eastern coast of what is today Tunisia. He remained there long enough to settle his family before setting out to follow his dream of becoming a famous court poet. His first success was realized when he was invited to join the court of al-Mu'tamid ibn 'Abbad, king of the petty kingdom (*ta'ifa*) of Seville. There he remained until 1091 when the Berber Almoravid forces launched their campaigns throughout al-Andalus, and forced al-Mu'tamid and members of his court into exile. Ibn Hamdis returned to the central North African province of Ifriqiya where he lived the entire second half of his life serving as court poet for the last four Zirid princes.

The standard Arabic historical archive yields very little information about Ibn Hamdis al-Siqilli (the Sicilian). Apart from a handful of entries in biographical dictionaries that list him as a highly skilled and celebrated poet and that cite selections from his verses about Sicily for which he was best known, there are no details on his education nor anything about what he may have written beyond poetry. Nonetheless, Ibn Hamdis survives in memory and in text through his vast collection of poems collated into an anthology (*diwan*) that contains 370 poems, ranging from long *qasida*-s to short two-line poems. It is the powerful autobiographical voice that can be heard, especially throughout the praise poems he penned to the powerful men he served, and to the elegies he composed to mourn beloved family members and friends that guides us to the biographical details of his life.

This book taps heavily into the poetry. There are over two dozen poems that I have chosen to help me tell the story of Ibn Hamdis's extraordinary life, lived in turbulent but 'interesting' times. In the early chapters, I cite the poems in full translations (all are mine unless otherwise indicated) in order to give my reader as strong a sense possible of the man and the poem. Ibn Hamdis was conservative in his faithful adherence to the conventions and strictures of classical Arabic poetry, but very much (may I say?) modern in the ways he could manipulate the conventions to display a creative intertextuality and poetic inventiveness to convey meaning and relevance to a whirlwind of contemporaneous political events taking place in a highly dynamic medieval Muslim Mediterranean world. In cases where the poem is lengthy and cited in full translation, I walk my reader through what I see as constituent parts (or movements) of the poem, since they carry with them layers of meaning not immediately apparent to a non-specialist. The sequencing, for example, of an amatory or gnomic preface, followed by a scene of departure or an arduous journey across hostile terrain, and finally a segment of praise or eulogy, follows the conventions set by the pre-Islamic Arabian ode, but bear rich significance to the message or the occasion of the poem. In poems of the later chapters, I choose to forgo full translations, deleting in particular verses that are overly formulaic and repetitive, and I cite those verses in which the autobiographical voice is most clearly audible. In other words, I provide Ibn Hamdis himself many occasions to tell his own story.

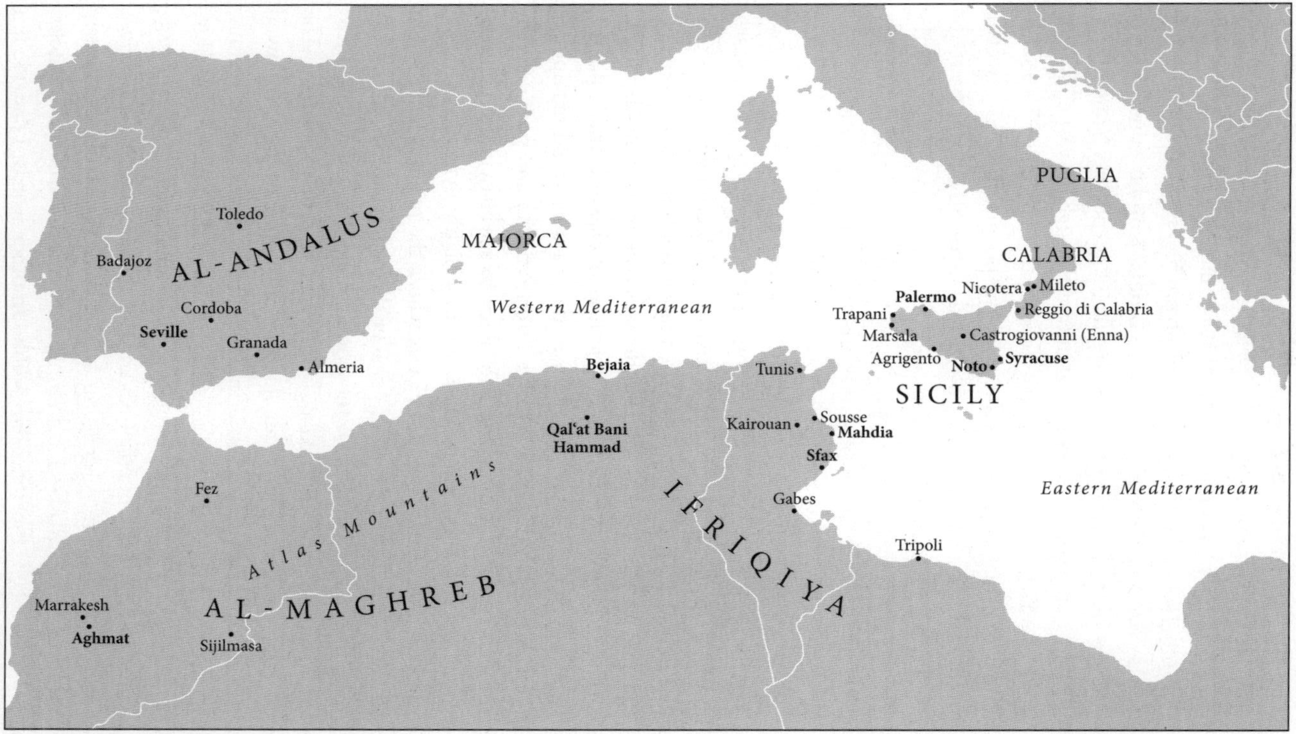

Ibn Hamdis's World

1

BORN UNDER A BAD SIGN

On a blustery winter Mediterranean night in the mid eleventh century, in the eastern province of the island of Sicily, Ibn al-Thumna engaged in a heated discussion with his wife, Umm Ibrahim. In a fit of rage, he assaulted her, then called out to have her veins bled, leaving her to die. Her son, Ibrahim, being a witness to this, summoned the doctors who arrived in time to save her life. On the following morning, Ibn al-Thumna, nursing a hangover and experiencing feelings of guilt, pleaded for his wife's forgiveness, making as his excuse his state of intoxication. His wife accepted his apologies. In the weeks to follow, most likely taking advantage of her husband's lingering state of repentance, she asked his permission to travel to visit her brother, to which he assented.

It just so happened that the island of Sicily by this time had been carved up and was ruled by three petty warlords, one of whom was Umm Ibrahim's husband, and the second her brother. Ibn al-Thumna, controlled the cities of Syracuse and Catania, along with their adjacent areas, and her brother, ʿAli ibn Niʿma, better known as Ibn al-Hawwas, ruled the central cities and adjacent areas of Castrogiovanni (modern Enna) and Agrigento. The third warlord, ʿAbdallah ibn Mankut, carved out his fiefdom around the cities of Mazara and Trapani located on the western part of the island. The city of Palermo, long the political and military capital of Muslim Sicily, was slowly slipping away from the hands of the last Kalbid princes who had ruled the island since the middle of the tenth century.

When the seemingly forgiving wife, whom some sources name as Maymuna, arrived at her brother's castle, she wasted little time in revealing to him what had transpired between her and her husband.

In a furious and indignant reaction, Ibn al-Hawwas refused to allow his sister to return to her husband. After repeated messages inquiring about his wife's delay and receiving no replies, Ibn al-Thumna assembled a militia. Ibn al-Thumna by now was emerging as the most powerful of the three warlords, having gained a vast amount of territory and even having his name pronounced at Friday sermons in the cathedral mosque in Palermo. With confidence and the flexed muscle of his own militia, he set out along with his troops and surrounded the main fortress in Castrogiovanni. Its powerful occupant, Ibn al-Hawwas, responded with an attack with his own militia and succeeded not only in breaking Ibn al-Thumna's blockade but chasing him and whoever survived of his forces all the way back to Catania.

Having suffered the loss of many of his soldiers, Ibn al-Thumna, in an act of desperation and what would eventually amount to treason, resorted to the ultimate folly of seeking the assistance of the Norman battalions that had recently been making inroads on the island and were at this time camping on the outskirts of the city of Mileto, in the northeast corner of the island. The Normans, having set their sights on Sicily for some time, were only too willing to come to his aid. In 1052, they marched with the forces of Ibn al-Thumna and surrounded the castle of Castrogiovanni. This time, Ibn al-Hawwas was unable to put up much of a resistance.

THE KALBIDS OF SICILY

The island of Sicily since the last decades of the tenth century had been reaping the fruits of the Muslim conquest of the island that began in the second decade of the ninth century. The dynasty of the Banu Kalb, or the Kalbids, achieved a significant degree of autonomous rule in Sicily by the mid tenth century. The Kalbids had been active players in the Maghreb since Umayyad times of the eighth century, in both administrative and military roles. Although they lost much of their influence during the Banu al-Aghab (Aghlabids) reign of Ifriqiya (801–909), they re-emerged when the Fatimids came to power in 909. They supported the early Fatimid caliphs and were rewarded for their loyalty and military prowess with appointments as governors, judges, and provincial tax collectors throughout the island. Their influence and power increased there, especially after the Fatimids moved their headquarters to Egypt (972), leaving their [central] North African territories in the hands of loyal but rivalling factions.

Abu al-Futuh Yusuf ibn ʻAbdallah al-Kalbi, nicknamed *Thiqat al-Dawla* (Trust of the Realm), was appointed governor of Sicily by the Fatimid caliph in Egypt, al-ʻAziz, and ruled the island from 989–998. The medieval Arab historians are in agreement that Yusuf's reign represented a high point in the history of Muslim Sicily. During his time, the Sicilian jihad, the project to conquer, colonize, and Islamicize the island with all the adornments of Muslim culture and civilization, was back on track after bouts on internal dissent and rebellion, and the island was prospering from political stability, economic prosperity, and the reaping of the first harvests of an indigenous 'Sicilian' Arab-Muslim cultural production. The borders were relatively secured against any Byzantine or other external interferences, and more and more Christian towns, especially in the northeast corner of the island, were submitting to Islamic dominance and rule.

But the daggers of Fate, that oft-cited villain of classical Arabic poetry, were flashed onto the island when Yusuf was smitten with a stroke that left half of his body paralyzed. Unable to continue to rule, he appointed his oldest son, Jaʻfar, to replace him. The son continued to rule in the same vein of the father until his own brother ʻAli, the second son of Yusuf, rebelled against him with the collaboration of Berber and black slave factions of the army. Jaʻfar responded by dispatching his militias and succeeded in killing many of the rebelling soldiers. In the course of the battle, ʻAli was captured, taken prisoner, and executed a mere week after the rebellion erupted. The enraged Jaʻfar rounded up as many Berber soldiers he could seize and exiled them to North Africa, and he had as many of the slave corps he could find executed.

MUSLIM SICILY UNRAVELING

The army, now thinned out and consisting mainly of 'Sicilian' soldiers, that is, professional men of war who were sons and grandsons of the first generations of Muslim warriors and settlers, became emboldened, and they soon flexed their muscle by dethroning Ja'far. What had been the legacy of his father Yusuf in uniting Sicilian Muslims and bringing peace and prosperity to the island was at this time being torn asunder. Ja'far had fallen out of favor with his subjects for his heavy-handed rule, the arrogance he directed toward his brothers, his contempt for regional and religious leaders and, above all, his overbearing tax policies that turned large segments of the population against him. The year was 1019 when Ja'far was escorted out to public trial to face the charges against him. The elderly and incapacitated father, Yusuf, then appeared, carried on a stretcher, to plead on his son's behalf. Our chroniclers described how the masses cried out their sympathy and affection for their infirm former ruler, and then complained bitterly of his son's abuses of power. A despondent and contrite Yusuf consented to their request to remove him, and soon thereafter the paralyzed father and disgraced son gathered much of their massive fortune and departed to the safety and protection of their Fatimid patrons in Egypt.

Yusuf's third son, Ahmad ibn Yusuf al-Akhal, so-called for his dark complexion, quite possibly being the son of an African mother, was acclaimed as the new governor, testament to the continuous staunch loyalty the Sicilians harbored for the house of Yusuf, and he ruled them for the next seventeen years. Perhaps in a burst of religious zeal, or merely to divert attention from the smoldering residue of the recent domestic disturbances, or possibly in his quest to refill his coffers with badly needed funds to be gained by the spoils of war, al-Akhal resumed an aggressive jihad campaign, launching attacks against Christian towns in Calabria and Puglia on the Italian mainland, looting and taking prisoners, and even pillaging Sicilian towns whose loyalties he held in suspicion.

Al-Akhal's strategies of ruling a once-again fractious Sicilian population, however, proved in the long run to be disastrous. By the time he assumed power, the deepest cleavage in the island's population was no longer the Arab/Berber divide, but one between what the Arab historians came to designate as 'Sicilian' versus 'North African.' The Sicilians were those people, Arab and Berber alike, who conquered and settled this island, bringing Arabic and Islam onto as much of it as they could. As scions, sons and daughters, of the early generations of *mujahidun*, they were landowners, farmers or urban dwellers, military or civilian, who came to consider Sicily their *homeland*. The North Africans were relative newcomers, hundreds, if not thousands, mainly from the Kutama and Sanhaja Berber tribes of the central Maghreb, who arrived on the island during Fatimid rule as military recruits—or perhaps as political exiles— in search of opportunities for a better life. But Sicily was only so big and its resources so vast, and the opportunities available to the earlier Muslim arrivals were no longer as abundant to the newcomers. To many of the locals, they must have been seen as 'foreign,' even though they were Muslims. But their military might was still very much needed to repel Muslim Sicily's external enemies, increasing steadily especially on its northern borders.

Taking advantage of this growing rift, al-Akhal summoned the leaders of the 'Sicilian' population and proposed to them that he rid the island of these 'North Africans.' Much to his surprise, no doubt, they refused, saying that these people were by now related to them through marriage. He dismissed them, and then summoned the leaders of the North Africans with the same proposal. This time, having nothing to lose and much to gain, they agreed. Al-Akhal then ordered that their possessions be protected, and that stiff taxes be imposed on the Sicilians. As expected, all hell broke loose.

The chaos that followed on the island was of grave concern to al-Mu'izz ibn Badis (r. 1017–1062), the autonomous Zirid governor of Ifriqiya. Since the departure of the Fatimids to Egypt, the Sanhaja Berber Zirid family gained control over much of the central Maghreb, and to reinforce their own influence, they resumed Ifriqiya's active interest and intervention into Sicilian affairs. So when a group of Sicilians sailed to the Zirid headquarters in Mahdia (*al-Mahdiyya*) for their assistance against the al-Akhal government, al-Mu'izz responded with a heavily manned and armed flotilla commanded by his own son. When it arrived at the al-Khalisa, the citadel near the port in Palermo, the Zirids, witnessing the chaos and divisions, departed soon thereafter, and in the ensuing mayhem al-Akhal was killed. Neither the good intentions of the Zirid Court nor the acclamation of Hasan al-Simsam,

Yusuf's fourth son, as governor of Sicily, could salvage the deterioration of Muslim Sicily.

Amid such chaos, the three warlords mentioned above seized the moment and rose to power. And, it was during these hard times, roughly in the year 1055, when Ibn Hamdis was born.

BORN IN SYRACUSE, BECOMING A POET

Abu Muhammad 'Abd al-Jabbar ibn Abu Bakr ibn Muhammad Ibn Hamdis was born in the city of Syracuse (in the southeast province of Noto) in 1055 to a family of the Azdi tribe, who emigrated from the Arabian Peninsula to Syria and then crossed over to North Africa at the end of the first Islamic century. His father, Abu Bakr, and his grandfather Muhammad, were most likely the descendants of military commanders who, by the time of his birth, had settled as landed gentry in the southeast corner of the island. The first generations of *mujahidun* coming to Sicily began to arrive from North Africa, more precisely from the central province of Ifriqiya (today consisting of all of Tunisia, eastern Algeria and western Libya). The 'conquest' of Sicily was the project of the Aghlabid dynasty who ruled Ifriqiya from 801 to 909. They were granted rulership of these recently conquered lands by the 'Abbasid caliphate in Baghdad, in part due to their military successes, and in part due to the difficulties the 'Abbasids would face in governing such a distant province. Baghdad's recognition of their 'autonomy' extracted an annual sum of 40,000 dinars and continuous pledges of allegiance to the 'Abbasid caliphate.

In 827, Ziyadat-Allah I, the third Aghlabid prince (emir), launched a full-scale invasion against Byzantine Sicily with all the pomp and pageantry of an Islamic jihad, not so much as an act of religious duty than a political solution to the many social, political, and economic problems he was facing at home. On a June morning in 827, the commander of the Aghlabid fleet, Asad ibn al-Furat, stood at the port of Sousse (*Susa*) on the eastern '*sahil*' of what is today's east coast of Tunisia. A scholar of Islamic law and a recently appointed chief judge of the city of Kairouan (al-Qayrawan), Asad was named to command the invasion that would eventually lead to the Arab Islamic colonization of Sicily. He addressed his soldiers and the thousands of spectators who had gathered to witness the spectacle in Quranic terms. Ziyadat-Allah's army was ethnically and professionally diverse; it consisted of Arabs and Berbers, Persians, and Africans; and it included professional soldiers (senior officers and recruits), slaves, medics, and religious scholars, preachers and teachers alike. The copious classical Arabic biographical literature unfortunately leaves us no clue as to where we may trace Ibn Hamdis's origins among these first arrivals. We have no idea whether his grandfather or father pursued professional careers or scholarly ones.

'Abd al-Jabbar Ibn Hamdis nonetheless remains today as the best-known figure from the Arabo-Muslim period of medieval Sicily. Perhaps the Norman court geographer, Abu 'Abdallah Muhammad al-Idrisi (c. 1100–1165), author of the famous *Book of Roger*, shares equal fame in the eyes of many. Ibn Hamdis carries relatively scant personal information in medieval Arabic biographical literature. There is no mention of his education, teachers, or students, nor is there much on the details of his personal or professional life other than brief citations of his poetry with short commentaries. He is cited in numerous later sources but, again, most of the entries are brief. Ibn Hamdis's fame rests solely on his extant diwan that contains 370 pieces (amounting to well over six thousand verses), ranging from two-line poems to full-length *qasida*-s (odes) as long as 80 lines, as previously mentioned. The survival of this diwan, as opposed to the much shorter one of his compatriot, Abu al-Hasan 'Ali al-Bilanubi, and the hundreds of fragments of poetry by Arab Sicilian poets that survived in larger anthologies, has bestowed on Ibn Hamdis enduring fame and unique literary stature in both classical Arabic literature and in Muslim Sicilian history. The sheer size of the diwan attests to his long and prolific career. The diversity of its genres, panegyric (*madih*), elegy (*ritha'*), love poem (*ghazal*), devotional poem (*zuhdiyya*), wine song (*khamriyya*), and description (*wasf*) underscores his artistic versatility. The preponderance of the panegyric, from his earlier days at the 'Abbadid court in Seville to his twilight years at the Zirid court at Mahdia, calls attention to a career intrinsically tied to and financially and professionally dependent upon the political whims and winds of his time.

However, above and beyond the size and condition of the diwan, and its uniqueness in the literary history of Muslim Sicily, Ibn Hamdis's poetry scintillates in its power to capture the historical moment, when the politics, culture, aesthetics, and states of mind and emotions are brought to light through his particular vision of the world. If rearranged chronologically, Ibn Hamdis's diwan could be read, as I have argued elsewhere, as a 'diary in verse' in which the intimate details of his life and his emotional stances toward the people and events that shaped it give voice to those precarious and unpredictable times in which he lived. In fact, an attempted chronology of Ibn Hamdis's life experiences has been as much a subject of modern scholarly inquiry as has been his poetic oeuvre: curious, given the fact that so little of his life has been recorded in the conventional sources of the Arabic archive, biographical dictionaries, anthologies, and *adab* (belles-lettrist) writings. Yet the bits and pieces of historical information in his poetry, allusions to actual events, descriptions of real people and places, pieced together, create an archive from which we can tell his life story.

The year in which Ibn Hamdis was born coincided with the ongoing fragmentation of the island and the usurpation of power by the three petty warlords mentioned above, as well as the initial military successes of the Normans on the island. The combination of both of these, as we have seen and will see again, was responsible for waves of evacuation of especially the island's Muslim elite. Despite the political deterioration, ironically, it was also a period when Muslim Sicilians were reaping the benefits of previous generations' economic and material development as well as scholarly and artistic production.

EDUCATION IN AN EARLY JIHADI FRONTIER

We can safely assume that Ibn Hamdis was provided with a 'conventional' Muslim education. Given the fact that he was male (and most likely the oldest or only son), and that he hailed from a family of comfortable means, he studied in a primary school where he learned reading and writing, scriptures (Quran and hadith) and Arabic grammar and philology. In the absence of any normative biographical information accorded to scholars and men of high culture (poets included) in the classical Arabic period, one can also imagine the broad strokes of the intellectual landscape in which Ibn Hamdis was raised. His own diwan, a vast encyclopedia of historical, linguistic, and philological knowledge, and an immensely rich terrain of poetic intertextuality and inventiveness, had to come from somewhere.

Much of the genius in Ziyadat-Allah's decision to launch a jihad against Byzantine Sicily lay in his inclusion of religious scholars among the combatants. Not only did it reinforce the legitimacy and sanctity of what at the time was deemed by many of the Qayrawani jurists (*'ulama'*) to be a violation of a cease-fire treaty that was still in effect between the Aghlabids of Ifriqiya and the Byzantine government of Sicily, it was very much a tactical investment in a project that had long-term possibilities. Any conquered land, by force or by submission, would need to be settled quickly, and mosques, schools, courts, and residences would need to be built, not only for the retired soldiers and their families, but for the newly converted as well. The composition of such a diverse invading army would and did serve this purpose.

The first century of the Sicilian jihad was, as expected, spent on military operations. Most of the manpower and resources were directed onto the battlefield. The heavy resistance from both local Christian Sicilian populations, supported by local monasteries and the papacy, as well as from their Byzantine occupiers, required extensive and relentless efforts on the part of the invading forces, not to mention a constant flow of reinforcements (soldiers and weapons) from Ifriqiya. It is in this first century when the co-dependence of North Africa and Sicily takes deep root and, as we have seen, it endured throughout Muslim Sicilian history, right up to and including the Zirid princes' last attempts to salvage the island from the Norman conquest two hundred years after their first landing. This relationship was one not only of a political/military nature, but also a religious and intellectual/cultural one as well.

Muslim Sicilian scholars make their first appearance in late-tenth- and early eleventh-century biographical dictionaries. They are, in the main, men who resemble closely their counterparts in the 'motherland' of Ifriqiya, and who are primarily trained in the Maliki school of [Sunni] Islamic law. These first generation 'Sicilian' scholars were specialists in the Quranic sciences (exegesis, recitations, etc.), Prophetic hadith, jurisprudence, and Arabic language and philology. Their genealogies span a wide range of *nisba*-s, i.e., indications of origin, being sons of families who traced their roots to various parts of the Islamic world, most often from areas of the wider North Africa (*al-maghrib*) but also from cities and towns in greater Syria and Mesopotamia (*al-mashriq*), or to various tribes, Arab as well as Berber.

The inclusion of religious scholars and teachers in the jihad's invading army would extend well into the first century with a constant flow of appointments, political, military, juridical, and scholarly, made directly from the rulership in Ifriqiya. To a great degree the development of religious, social, and scholarly (read: civil) institutions in Sicily was a carbon copy of what was happening across the sea. The triumph of the Maliki jurists over their Hanafi Sunni rivals was replicated in Sicily by way of Maliki trained scholars who migrated to Sicily as teachers, judges, and chaplains, and who taught Maliki authored and sanctioned texts. In the course of time, the gradual development of urban centers (beginning with Palermo), the settlement of retired *mujahidun*, and the birth of new generations who opted for scholarly and not military careers, broadened the scope of intellectual activity and production.

By the late-tenth and early to middle decades of the eleventh century, Muslim Sicilian Arabic bio-bibliography advanced in ways that reflected developments taking place not only in the major centers of the wider Maghreb (including al-Andalus), but in the Islamic East as well. This advancement in Sicilian Muslim intellectual life was, in sum, based on a number of factors; the development of urban centers and their institutions of learning; the gradual evolution of Muslim Sicilian society from an exclusively military or 'ghazi' one to a more diverse (read: civil) one with citizens pursuing careers in education, trade, the arts and crafts; and greater exposure to external influences, from academic study-abroad (*rihla*), to commerce, and pilgrimage to Mecca.

THE RISE OF AN INDIGENOUS MUSLIM-SICILIAN CULTURE

Scholars and scholarship from Baghdad, Damascus, and Cairo flashed on the Sicilian radar screen, providing texts to study and models to emulate. Islamic law as an intellectual discipline expanded out into its various branches, Sufism was on the rise, and works of *adab* (belles-lettres) and other genres of expository writing were flourishing. Poetry, a key sub-field in the study of Arabic philology, had become as much a field of linguistic and philological inquiry as it was a popularly practiced art form. The massive treasure trove of *jahili* (pre-Islamic) poetry and the rise of the *badi*' (rhetorical embellishment) style, favored by many of the 'modernist' poets of the early 'Abbasid period, continued to inspire Sicilian poets to emulate 'the classics' and to create their own indigenous *Sicilian Arabic* verse. A new generation of rising Sicilian poets, like their Andalusian counterparts, relished their mastery of the poetic canons and strove to compete with the poetic giants of the Arab east.

In his own times, Ibn Hamdis would have knowledge of and indeed access to some of the most outstanding literary and linguistic scholars of the greater Maghreb, Sicily included. The archive has preserved for us sketches of some of the most eminent among them. I cite them not with any attempt to draw connections between them and Ibn Hamdis, but to sketch a picture of Sicilian scholarly production at the time:

Abu Bakr Ibn al-Birr (d. 1068) was specialist in grammar who authored texts on grammar and lexicography. He studied in the Arab East and settled in Sicily. We know that when he was expelled from Mazara for his excessive drinking, he made his way to the more liberal and cosmopolitan climate of Palermo; Abu 'Ali Hasan Ibn Rashiq (d. 1071), literary scholar from Kairouan and poet at the court of the Zirid prince, al-Mu'izz Ibn Badis, was the author of the highly influential *Kitab al-'Umda*, an encyclopedia of sorts for classical Arabic poetry and poetics. He fled to Sicily (for reasons unknown) where he spent the last years of his life; 'Umar ibn Khalaf Ibn Makki (d. 1107) was a scholar of Quran and hadith who came to specialize in Arabic grammar and dialectology. His unique *Tathqif al-lisan fi Talqih al-Janan* (Educating the Tongue and Cultivating the Heart), a book on Sicilian Arabic, including idioms, provincialisms, and common linguistic errors made by the general public, is a remarkable example of how much Arabic linguistic studies in Sicily advanced beyond classical Quranic philology; 'Ali ibn Ja'far Ibn al-Qatta' (d. 1122) was a student of Ibn al-Birr and is best remembered for a massive encyclopedia he composed on Sicilian poets and poetry; and last, 'Abd al-Rahman Ibn al-Fahham (d. 1122) combined all the best of Arabic philology, delving into the complexities of Quranic morphology and syntax. Unlike Ibn Hamdis, who dedicated himself solely to poetry, all of these scholars, it should be noted, composed their own verses in addition to their 'academic' writings. But like Ibn Hamdis, most of them left Sicily at the time of the Norman invasions and settled in either Ifriqiya, al-Andalus, or Egypt.

POETRY IN MUSLIM SICILY, FROM PHILOLOGY TO ART AND POLITICS

The sketches above comprise a small but illuminating picture of literary-cultural life in Muslim Sicily at the time of its political deterioration. Beyond the biographies of these men of high scholarly achievement lies a gallery of personalities of high culture or high social standing who composed poetry, as professionals or dilettantes. The Arab Sicilian archive yields literally dozens of names of Sicilians from various walks of life who tried their hand at composing verse. Unfortunately, their work survives only in fragments cited in later anthologies as examples of their best work. These would-be poets were in the main scholars of Islamic theology and law, philologists and grammarians, writers of polite prose (*udaba'*), and in some cases merchants, high-ranking soldiers, and bureaucrats, and even princes from the ruling family.

Poetry, as both an academic discipline and a cultural phenomenon, was widely composed, practiced, and performed during Muslim Sicily's 'golden age' under the Kalbid dynasty. The growth and florescence of a Kalbid court produced a corps of highly literate functionaries with a command of literary Arabic needed to serve the government's needs. The drafting of official documents, royal edicts, diplomatics, legal rulings, commercial, and other kinds of treaties and transactions required opening secretarial schools (*diwan insha'*) that would train scribes and other secretarial staff to compose Arabic at its highest register. After the Quran, classical Arabic poetry served as something of a collective textbook to educate these students by exposing them to all the best of Arabic vocabulary, grammar, and stylistics. At a time and place when rhetorical embellishment (*badi'*) was in vogue, no better models of high literacy were found than in the poetic canons that provided examples of the many figures of speech, punning, metaphor, simile, alliteration, etc., all the de rigueur tools for a cultivated scribe or bureaucrat.

The culture of the medieval Mediterranean Court, whether Arabic Muslim, Greek Byzantine, or Latin West, as elsewhere in the Muslim East for that matter, extended beyond the quotidian workings of government offices and extended well into the evenings of male-bonding and professional and social (read: political) networking. The hunting lodges and pleasure palaces of the ruling elite, as well as of men of high social or military standing, served as sites for usually nocturnal entertainment where 'wine, women, and song' were celebrated in the company of professional court poets. Handsomely paid and fiercely competitive, these 'hired hands' used their poetic skills and talents to lavish praise on a powerful patron. Their poetry required inventiveness, often improvisation, and a credibility that suited the occasion. Whether celebrating a military victory (or disguising a military defeat), or extending congratulations on a holiday or the circumcision of a son, toasting a ruler or patron in verse required not only profound knowledge and command of the classical Arabic panegyric tradition, but the ability to persuade the recipient of praise as well as the members of his entourage of the sincerity and credibility of the poem. Arabic poetry, after all, was a widespread cultural phenomenon and a public affair, and very often with potential political bite. Both the composition and the performance of an Arabic panegyric were most effective at festive occasions on which large audiences with highly refined poetic tastes and expectations gathered.

Ibn Hamdis composed a short, ten-line poem in the form of a wine song (*khamriyya*) in which he describes a physical setting that captures the atmosphere and mood of male bonding on one such occasion. In it he incorporates many of the favorite images and tropes that had come to create the climate of nocturnal court culture:

1 I remember a certain brook that offered the impiety of drunkenness to the topers
[sitting] along its course, with [its] cups of golden [wine].
2 Each silver cup in it filled as though it contained
the soul of the sun in the body of the full moon.
3 Whenever a glass reached anyone in our company of topers,
he would grasp it gingerly with his ten fingers.
4 Then he drinks out of it a grape-induced intoxication
which lulls his very senses without his realizing it.
5 He sends [the glass] back in the water, thus returning it
to the hands of the cupbearer at whose will it had [originally] floated [to him].
6 Because of the wine bibbing we imagined our song to be melodies
which the birds sang without verse,
7 While our cupbearer was the water which brought [us wine] without a hand,
and our drink was a fire that shone without embers,
8 And which offered us delights of all kinds, while the only reward [of that cupbearer]
for [giving us those delights] was that we offered him to the ocean to drink.
9 [It is] as if we were cities along the riverbank
while the wine-laden ships sailed [the stretch] between us.
10 For life is excusable only when we walk
along the shores of pleasure and abandon all restraint!

(Diwan #199: 193; translated by James Monroe)

CRAFTING A POETICS OF 'HOMELAND'

Ibn Hamdis has bequeathed to Islamic civilization, to Arabic literature, and to Sicilian history a prodigious anthology of his poetry that abounds in many landmarks and milestones that allow us to sketch the contours of his long and circuitous life. The value of this anthology rests on two pillars of distinction: the first is an encyclopedic depository that preserves a philological treasure trove of lexical, linguistic, historical, and cosmological information from the universal to the minute; and the second is its monumental and eternal tribute to his beloved homeland, Sicily. The anthology is the product of the experience of living in a time and in a place where the art and artistry of classical Arabic poetry was very much alive and appreciated. It was a place situated on the outskirts or, as the medieval Arabs referred to it, as the frontier (*al-thaghr*), of a massive Islamic Empire that could boast centuries of stellar literary and intellectual achievements, and where artists and scholars living on the periphery aspired to be 'more Catholic than the Pope,' as modern parlance would have it. Yet it was a time when the Islamic world had splintered into petty kingdoms and principalities, and the lands of the Islamic frontier were being pushed behind the lines of defense against a growing offensive by a surging Christian conquest.

Ibn Hamdis's poetic oeuvre is imbued with centuries of Arabo-Islamic knowledge and lore: philological (linguistic), historical, and environmental. His philology was wide and deep. He commanded a massive vocabulary that included archaic words, idiomatic expressions, adages, and proverbs. As part of the 'neo-classical' school of Arabic poetry which won favor especially among poets of Muslim Spain (*al-Andalus*) and Sicily, Ibn Hamdis mastered the canons of pre-Islamic (*jahiliyya*) poets as well as the post-Islamic (Umayyad and 'Abbasid) poetry especially of the modernist *badi'* movement, bringing into his poems an intricate weaving of intertextuality with Arabic poetry's masterpieces. His uncanny skill in creating metaphoric language, at times, admittedly, with a heavy hand, allowed him to manipulate other figures of speech that provided him with a language to express personal and at times esoteric sentiments in a highly mannered and public poetry.

In addition to his expansive literary and linguistic prowess, Ibn Hamdis demonstrated throughout his poems a vast knowledge of history and a sophisticated historical consciousness.

His many allusions and references to ancient Near Eastern cultures, Zoroastrian and Sassanian Iranian, biblical Hebrew, early Christian, pre-Islamic Arabian, and Islamic, from the time of the Prophet Muhammad to his own, contributed richly to that encyclopedic quality of his poetry. His ability and willingness to draw from Yemeni tribal history, narrate the battles of the Prophet Muhammad against his Meccan adversaries, and etch sketches of the heroes and villains of the early wars of conquest that brought Islam and Arabic into the newly conquered territories of Mesopotamia, Syria, Egypt, and North Africa not only gave his poetry broad historical and geographical dimension, but provided him with the tools to coin his own vocabulary and fashion wide frames of reference which he would skillfully manipulate in describing and explicating the ups and downs of his own turbulent times.

Third, Ibn Hamdis's poetry is steeped in a powerful sense of place and of the environment in which he lived. It reflects a cosmological-physical knowledge and understanding of the celestial and natural sciences, and a love and appreciation for the natural world. Especially through the poetic genre of description (*wasf*), which had become fashionable among the neoclassical poets of medieval Muslim Spain and Sicily, he composed his verses rich in meteoric images of planets, moons, and stars, following the traditions of the Arabian poets of the Jahiliyya, as well as of clouds, rain storms, and lightning. His descriptive verses obsess with seas, rivers, brooks, and streams, and with mountains, valleys, pastures, orchards, and flowers, not to mention the hundreds of verses that describe the desert in all its terrifying vastness and awesome majesty. As we will see, the desert will become a dominant metaphor in the poet's life experiences of crossing through hostile terrain as he lived his life in exile, keeping with Arab poetic tradition but breathing contemporary and personal meaning into it.

Ibn Hamdis's poetry also celebrates the animal world, a reflection of his 'environmental consciousness,' to borrow a modern term. His many verses on horses and camels can be read intertextually with the giants on ancient Arabian poetry as venerated figures of authentic Arabian beauty and as vehicles on which the poet makes his arduous journeys through life. Ibn Hamdis's description poems include the lion, giraffe, wolf, wild cow, and birds of various species; the hawk, eagle, dove, canary, ostrich, and sand grouse. He even composed a poem describing a falcon hunting seagulls. His sensitivity to his physical environment is whimsically illustrated in a brief four-line poem about insects:

1 Atop of my mattress, my sleep is disturbed,
 and this increases throughout the night.
2 There are those who come to visit like yawning wolves
 that crawl up quickly and lie in wait.
3 They turn my blood into wine and take turns drinking,
 finding the prices of what is dear to be cheap.
4 You see gnats singing to the tune of a fiddle,
 while the bed bugs imbibe and the fleas dance.
(Diwan #172: 289)

This poem, a rare display of a sense of humor, demonstrates the poet's powerful poetic impulse especially in expressing personal discomfort or grief. It takes the form of a wine song and he injects it with music and nocturnal imagery. His own body suffers insomnia and his blood is turned into wine, suggesting a possible reference to the image of Christ's transubstantiation. It allows the poet to commune with his immediate environment, even with the lowliest of God's creatures. When read against his entire poetic production, its most poignant meaning points to life on the road, in a desert tent or a modest inn on a lonely road or remote mountain pass.

The existence and survival of this large anthology steeped in such linguistic, literary, and poetic bravura and lore is matched in its value by the deeply lyrical and intensely political messages of love and devotion to a homeland. Rare it is, indeed, that we find in pre-modern Arabic literature such a life-long commitment—Ibn Hamdis lived well into his eighties—to a single place or a land. In the year 1078, the young aspiring poet fled his beloved homeland. The island was irreparably fractured, and the forces under the command of the Norman Roger I had taken effective control of Palermo (c. 1072). He was twenty-four, and he departed his hometown of Syracuse, which itself would fall in 1086, in the province of Noto and headed toward the city of Sfax (*Safaqus*), most likely with the intention, or perhaps just the hope, of returning one day.

That was not to be. Fate determined that he would never return home. His long life in exile, as agonizing as it was, did bring him success in achieving his goal of becoming a professional court poet. His diwan was the love child of both his exile and his professional accomplishments. He never forgot Sicily, and he seized every available opportunity to remember, remind, and lament his loss and Islam's loss to the Christians. By means of his poetic skill, he became Muslim Sicily's 'national' poet-in-exile, its itinerant memoirist, wandering minstrel, panegyrist and eulogist, chronicler, historian, town-crier, and holy warrior. The autobiographical voice heard from his verses never went mute, and for this he remains Muslim Sicily's premier citizen.

32 I remember Sicily, as agony stirs in my soul
all remembrances of her.
33 An abode for the pleasures of my youth that has been abandoned,
where once inhabited by the noblest of people.
34 For I have been vanished from Paradise,
and I [long to] tell you her story.
35 Were it not for the saltiness of tears
I would imagine my tears as her rivers.
36 I laughed at twenty years old out of youthful passion;
now at sixty I cry for her crimes.

(Diwan #110: 180–183)

2

DILEMMA: TO REMAIN OR DEPART

Two and a half centuries had passed between the time the Muslim forces set sail from the Ifriqiyan port of Sousse and landed at the Sicilian port of Mazara in 827 and the time when Ibn Hamdis departed from his beloved homeland in 1078. We know virtually nothing about the westward journey he embarked on from Syracuse to Sfax. We do know that members of his immediate family preceded him, and the general assumption is that the family had still maintained ties to relatives from the motherland. The distance was not far, and in many ways Ibn Hamdis was not traveling to a 'foreign' country. The Islamic conquest of Sicily had established and maintained relations between the island and the central North African province of Ifriqiya, creating in essence a 'motherland and colony,' a relationship bearing similarities to eighteenth-century Britain and the colonial United States. The bonds that linked the two together were demographic, linguistic, political, economic, and cultural, and they endured until the final stages of the Norman conquest in 1091.

SOJOURN IN SFAX: MAINTAINING THE IFRIQIYA-SICILY CONNECTION

When Ibn Hamdis arrived in Sfax to reunite with his family, he most assuredly felt an intimate familiarity with the people. He knew their language, their religion, their customs, and habits. These were the very people who sent generations of their sons and their families to participate in Islam's holy war, as professional soldiers and recruits, merchants, laborers, artisans and craftsmen, jurists, and scholars of many fields. Sicily attracted North Africans more and more as it gradually evolved into something of a boomtown where fortunes could be made, careers could be built, and identities could be reinvented. The constant back-and-forth movement of people and goods between the 'mainland' and the 'colony' kept the two Mediterranean neighbors joined to the hip, despite periods of serious turbulence, until the abdication of the last Zirid prince, al-Hasan ibn 'Ali, in 1148.

In addition to the human traffic that crossed the small stretch of sea between Ifriqiya and Sicily, there was a shared language, faith, and culture. Whatever ethnic or tribal diversity existed in North Africa was replicated on the island, including Arabs and Berbers in all their tribal multiplicity, as well as Persians, Africans, and Slavs. The mission of a holy war reinforced religious observation and instruction, and the triumph of Sunni Maliki Islam in North Africa was for the most part imported into Sicily. The Arabic language served as a social and cultural unifier, and as much as Berber and other vernaculars remained realties in daily life, it continued to be nourished and expanded through theological and intellectual ties with the major centers and institutions of Ifriqiya.

The relationship, however, was never without its challenges. In fact, the idea of a jihad into Sicily was conceived in discord. When the Aghlabid Court was approached in early 827 by a renegade Byzantine admiral, known as Euphemius, with information—never confirmed in the historical records—that Muslim troops were being held as prisoners in violation of a treaty enacted between Sicily and Ifriqiya, Ziyadat-Allah seized the occasion to launch a jihad. Such an action would solve many of the problems the Aghlabid Court was facing. It would employ a restless army, bring much needed funds into the government coffers, and it would create the specter of religious and political legitimacy to a government facing relentless criticism for its decadent ways and unjust rule.

The problem of the treaty signed by Ziyadat-Allah's father, 'Abdallah ibn Ibrahim al-Aghlab, had become a bone of contention among the Court's inner circle of advisors. Arguing against an attack before receiving positive proof of Euphemius's claim was Abu Muhriz, chief justice of Kairouan, and a leading figure among the highly influential and widely popular Maliki jurists (*fuqaha'*) who were at once harsh critics of Aghlabid corruption and champions of the disenfranchised masses. Arguing forcibly in favor of the conquest was Kairouan's second chief judge, Asad ibn al-Furat.

ASAD IBN AL-FURAT: MUSLIM SICILY'S FOUNDING FATHER

Abu 'Abdallah Asad ibn al-Furat ibn Sinan was born in 761 in the eastern Mesopotamian province of Khurasan. When he was two years old he came to Kairouan with his father, a soldier in the Umayyad army. He began his formal studies, Quran, hadith, jurisprudence, etc., when he was eighteen years old, and following the custom of his time, he embarked on an academic journey (*rihla*) to the major centers of learning in the east. He first embarked in the Hejaz where he studied directly under Malik Ibn Anas (711–795), the eponymous founder of the Maliki school of [orthodox] Islamic law, and then traveled to Iraq to expand his legal studies under the tutelage of the disciples of Abu Hanifa (699–767), the eponymous founder of the Hanafi school of law. The third stop on his journey was to Egypt where he sat at the feet of the most eminent of hadith scholars. He returned to Kairouan with a collation of his notes taken during his lessons, culminating in a legal compendium, *al-Asadiyya*, that became an authoritative legal manual which would be taught throughout North Africa.

The spread of Asad's fame caught the attention of the Aghlabid Court. His tutelage under the highest authorities of both the Maliki and Hanafi schools of Islamic jurisprudence, and his proclivity to mix and match legal opinions across schools in making his own legal judgements, would come in handy at a time and place when the Maliki and Hanafi jurists were at one another's throats as they jockeyed for power and influence. His success in winning over the Aghlabid Court led to his appointment as a *second* chief judge of Kairouan, a practice most uncommon in Islamic legal and political circles of the time.

Percolating in the corridors of power in Kairouan was the simmering feud among the jurists, many of whom chose to follow the teachings of Malik and many others the teachings of Abu Hanifa. At the heart of the divide were current ideas promoted by *Mu'tazilism*, a rationalist movement that took root in Muslim speculative theology (*kalam*) and was embraced by members of the Hanafi circles. At the time, it was much favored by the 'Abbasid Court in Baghdad and therefore was adopted by the Aghlabids in emulation of their Baghdadi patrons and models. Many of Kairouan's Hanafi legal scholars, referred to in North African sources as "Iraquis," were sympathetic to Mu'tazili positions, such as divine anthropomorphism, free will, and the created Quran, and therefore faced bitter accusations from the Malikis of committing unlawful, legal innovation (*bid'a*), or even apostasy (*ridda/irtidad*). It has been suggested in modern historiography that the Hanafis represented a liberal, elitist approach to the law, while the Malikis upheld a more traditional and populist approach. This legal/doctrinal dispute would undoubtedly have ramifications in the way Islamic law would unfold in Sicily.

Perhaps the greatest threat to Ziyadat-Allah's government was a rebellion within the military led by a high-ranking general, Mansur al-Tunbudhi, who amassed a large number of followers with whom he succeeded in holding Ziyadat-Allah hostage in his fortress for over ten years, taking control, in effect, of the city of Kairouan and other major areas of Ifriqiya. In the course of the siege, both of Kairouan's chief judges were called upon to meet al-Tunbudhi at his military headquarters and negotiate a deal for the rebels to withdraw. As would be the case in the debates concerning an Islamic jihad on Sicily, Abu Muhriz is depicted as having wavered before an aggressive and threatening al-Tunbudhi, while Asad ibn al-Furat stood his ground. Following the departure of the judges from the camp, a battalion was assembled under the command of Asad, the rebel forces were soundly defeated, and Ziyadat-Allah regained full control over his realm. By adding military muscle to a stellar scholarly profile, Asad emerged as a hero and was rewarded with the appointment to lead the Sicilian [physical and spiritual] jihad.

The Ifriqiya-Sicily relationship, once on the ground, was put to the test early on. Near the end of a year after the first landing in

Mazara in 827, the Muslim forces faced several setbacks after their initial successes in making forays into the island. The sudden arrival of Byzantine reinforcements from Constantinople put the *mujahidun* into a defensive position. Realizing they were prevented from escaping by sea routes, they burned their ships and headed inland for safe cover. Then, the unexpected and untimely death of their commander, Asad ibn al-Furat, from an epidemic that struck the Muslim battalions forced the commanding officers, cut off from the rulership in Kairouan, to choose one of their own to take the lead. This 'election' of sorts did not sit well with the Aghlabid Court, and a replacement was dispatched immediately. In fact, this action taken by the troops on the ground to select their own commanders and then be rejected by the powers that be in Ifriqiya would repeat itself on numerous occasions, sowing seeds of mutual suspicion that would sprout from time to time into open hostilities.

The local Sicilian populace and the occupying Byzantine forces were not the only enemy facing the Muslim holy warriors. Divisions within the military ranks, assassinations of Muslim generals and other commanding officers, sometimes carried out by members of the sub-Saharan slave corps (*'abid*), and disputes among the Arab officers and Berber recruits divulged ruptures among the *mujahidun*. Also, as the military mission of the jihad gave way to pockets of settlement, local insurrections eventually rose to the surface exposing divergences in new local interests, such as the division of the spoils of war or appointments to minor positions within the rank and file.

The Fatimid Revolution in Ifriqiya in 909 brought down the Aghlabid dynasty and instituted a new caliphate in central North Africa. Apart from the obvious fact that the Fatimids were adherents of Shi'ism, they nonetheless succeeded in their mission (*da'wa*) by winning over many of the local population. It was particularly large swathes of the disenfranchised Kutama and Sanhaja Berber tribes who, being victims as second-class citizens under governments ruled by Arab elites, responded, at least at the outset, to Fatimid propaganda of justice and equality. The Fatimids took control at first by not stepping on too many Sunni Maliki toes, and it appears that at least some adherents of the Hanafi school joined their ranks, partly in sympathy with some of their doctrinal views, and partly as a reaction against Maliki abhorrence to innovative thinking. Once they secured their position in Ifriqiya, the Fatimid Court turned its attention to the Sicilian jihad which was, even by their own admission, a major Aghlabid success, as well as a source for potential military, political, and economic expansion. After a difficult start with some ill-advised or hasty appointments and Sicilian hostility, especially among Aghlabid loyalists, there prevailed a mutual acceptance and understanding of the Sicilian-Ifriqiyan co-dependent relationship and its benefits. The Sicilian jihad was back on track with virtually little divergence from its original trajectory.

IBN HAWQAL'S SICILIAN CHAPTER

In the year 973, Abu al-Qasim ibn 'Ali Ibn Hawqal, renowned Arab geographer, cartographer, and chronicler from Baghdad, arrived in Palermo on the last leg of a long excursion that began nearly thirty years prior. His sojourn on the island, at least according to the fragments of his diary that have survived, was limited to the city of Palermo and its suburbs. To this day it remains the most significant first-person eyewitness account of life on the ground in the Muslim era of Sicily. Two features of his 'Sicilian Chapter' provide precious information on the sociology of Muslim Sicilian Islam: the first is a mapping of the city of Palermo; and the second is a series of caustic remarks he makes about the local population.

Ibn Hawqal's description of Palermo, referred to at the time as '*al-Madina*' (The City), was made up of five contiguous but separate sections; the old Center (*Balarm*), later referred to as '*Cassaro*,' was the walled city that dates back to Phoenician and Roman times; *al-Khalisa*, today's 'Kalsa' neighbor, which was built with direct access to the sea by the Fatimids following widespread disturbances; *Harat al-Saqalib* (the Slav Quarter), populated by retired soldiers who as captives from the Dalmatian Coast, came to serve in multiple capacities in the military conquest of Sicily; *al-Hara al-Jadida* (the New Quarter); and *Harat Masjid Ibn Saqlab* (Quarter of the Mosque of Ibn Saqlab), in the Jewish Quarter (*al-Hara al-Yahudiyya*) adjacent to Old Palermo (Balarm).

Ibn Hawqal's description shows that by the late tenth century the urban fabric of Palermo, and perhaps later read as a metaphor for all of the urban centers of Muslim Sicily, was a replica of the major metropolises of the wider Muslim world: Cordoba, Kairouan, Cairo, Damascus, and Baghdad. It encompassed a population of various peoples and it evolved around a bustling economic and mercantile network that extended into the rural areas as well as throughout the wider Mediterranean.

Ibn Hawqal's account of Sicily comes with caustic remarks directed toward Muslim Sicilians. Apart from their dim-wittedness, to which he attributes their excessive consumption of raw onions, he questions their predilection for building and worshipping in their own private mosques, their cowardice in shirking their duty to fight in the jihad, and their reckless negligence in observing Muslim customs. He complains about freeloading Sicilians, whom he accuses of being unemployed teachers, who loiter around mosques and defame the honor of righteous women. He expresses horror during a visit to the outskirts of Palermo of finding Muslim men who not only marry non-Muslim women who raise their daughters as Christian, but who also neglect prescribed duties and customs of Islam.

The conquest, settlement, and colonization for *Dar al-Islam* (the Muslim world) of Sicily, the largest island in the Mediterranean and situated well within Christian terrain, was a major feather in Islam's cap and it undoubtedly captured the imagination of Muslims worldwide. When Ibn Hawqal arrived in 973 he clearly came with an image of a jihad society on the frontier of Islam, where every believer lived every moment of his/her life fighting the enemy on the battlefield and building a society that followed literally the precepts and dictates of the faith. His comments, at times exaggerated if not comical, are best read as a reaction to the disappointment he must have felt in encountering a place and time running contrary to his expectations. The irony is that Muslim Sicily was still very much in a state of holy war. The regions of the northeast had yet to submit to Islam, the Byzantine Court in Constantinople continued to inject reinforcements to their loyalists on the island, and Christian churches and monasteries, supported by the papacy, maintained their resistance to the faith of the occupiers. But the realities of daily life changed since those early days of the Islamic conquest. The predominance of the *lesser* 'physical jihad' that did, indeed, require every Muslim to remain fully engaged on the battlefield, eventually ceded ground to the *greater* 'spiritual jihad' where the necessities of 'empire building' changed the course from conquest to civilization.

IN THE SHADOW OF THE NORMAN CONQUEST

Given the fragmentation of Muslim Sicily at the time of his birth, Ibn Hamdis spent his childhood years under the black clouds of doom. Compounding the political deterioration of any unified Muslim government, this was also the time, as we have seen, of the first forays onto the island by the armies of the Norman Robert Guiscard (1015–1085), Duke of Apulia, and his brother, Roger Borso I (1031–1101), whose capture of Palermo in 1072 ultimately led to Roger's investiture as Count of Sicily by which he ruled from 1072 to 1101. Both Robert and Roger were members of the House of Hauteville, and their descendants continued to rule the island until 1194. It only seems logical, then, that the young Ibn Hamdis, reading the writing on the wall, would take the decision to leave, if only for the reason of providing safety for his family and himself. The nineteenth-century Sicilian historian, Michele Amari, has posited the suggestion, based upon his reading of several verses, that Ibn Hamdis was forced to depart from the island because of a failed amorous relationship with a local Christian girl. In weighing the historical evidence of the dire political climate against the impressionistic reading of skimpy and ambiguous verses, it stands to reason that Ibn Hamdis fled the island for security reasons. What he would have us believe, at least through our reading of verses he would compose later in life, was that the decision to leave carried with it an intention to return. However, the behemoth of Fate, that ominous villain of his poetry, had something else in mind.

The young 'Abd al-Jabbar was raised in an extended family of comfortable means. His father, Abu Bakr, was widowed when the young

'Abd al-Jabbar's mother died prematurely, leaving both her son and a younger daughter. Both children went to live with their grandfather, Muhammad, after Abu Bakr decided to marry a young Sicilian girl. The husband of his father's sister, Yusuf Ibn Abi al-Dar, had also died at a young age. Like his own immediate family, 'Abd al-Jabbar's paternal aunt had two children, a boy and a girl. They also went to live in the grandfather's home. The paternal aunt raised all four children under the vigilant eye and protective wing of a doting grandfather. We will learn later through his poems that his own sister married her first cousin, 'Ali Ibn Yusuf Ibn Abi al-Dar, who would grow to become a doctor, and that he himself, through the urging—perhaps pressure—of his grandfather and aunt, would marry his first cousin. Not unusual for the customs of the time, the four children grew up in the same household and became two married couples. As a mature man and a perennial exile, Ibn Hamdis would outlive some of them and other members of his family. The elegies he composed, to his father, his wife, his aunt, and a daughter and nephew, shed light, as we will see later, on the family, and also the long and painful emotional attachments to them that he would maintain as long as he lived.

Based on the reading of several lines in the poem, translated and cited in full below, Amari connects his departure from Sicily to separation from a young maiden.

1 My heart is sobbing and [my] honor weeps,
yet the object of my ultimate desire is so close to me.
2 If where I remain with a young maiden were barren,
then my journey into the wasteland would be fertile.
3 If my resolve was anything like my sword,
then I would be a man smitten by two blows.
4 Take my determination from the chill of indifference,
for my passion for the young ladies is akin to contempt.
5 Seize the reins and do not neglect the night journey of camels,
for we have a steady trot in reaching our goals that does not fall short.
6 For the twinkling of the stars in the highest skies
has both its rise and setting on their horizons.
7 If there were only twists of fortune in my resolve,
then [my] soul would see its striving and would be pleased.

8 Even if the noble man lacks the space of one land,
how many lands would there be for him in a space wide open?
9 If you clothe your resolve in a coat of mail,
and set your foot into a stirrup you would be all the wiser.
10 [You who] deny me my own resolve which I know only too well [I said],
then your enemy, O my dear one, is a friend to me.
11 Her tears trickled down her cheeks,
and her kohl looked like pearls soaked in water dyed in lapis lazuli.
12 The black ravens [of ill omen] warned of his departure, she said,
and he will spend his years in exile.
13 What would happen was what she predicted,
or was it that the unknown was not unknown to her?
14 To his day journeys, his determination, his nocturnal travel, and desert camels,
he added a fifth: a stake that has a sturdy thrust.
15 He shot an arrow and with single mindedness he struck [his] grief,
just like the one hand aims at the other and hits it right on the mark.
16 He set sail on a desert ship into the abyss of quicksilver,
and from the [rising] mirage a south wind rocked its two sides,
17 with camels guided contently throughout the journey,
as long as the cameleer repeats his melodious chants.
18 Whenever they are whiplashed and their hides bleed,
the one holding the whip steps up the pace of the gait they are keeping.
19 God holds in His hands the reins of sunset
which resemble the camels' halters when their [water] supply runs dry.
20 You see them full to the brim in fear, with no safety for them;
you see them and you have doubts about them when you set out to travel.
21 Then it seems as though you made a mistake in crossing the desert,
and you must seek God's forgiveness for that.

22 And when the sun scorches its herbage, you imagine the sand turning to ashes
from which suddenly a fire ignites.
23 Whereupon you see the sun-baked Taurus
as though it were bearing the marks of an inferno caused by [your] fault.
24 The sounds of a screeching cry rising from it is like a plea,
when one of its flames catches the bowels on fire.
25 You suppose that this wasteland (desert) has been struck with fever,
and its water has turned into a torrent of sweat pouring forth.
26 But it is nothing more than a treasure
for a sand grouse and a wolf who both see it as the last breaths of life.
27 There is a chameleon whose face has not been singed by the scorching sun,
nor does it bear any sign of paleness because of it.
28 It has a water-wheel in its eye that does not turn for a thirsty man
when the water flows around him [but he cannot drink].
29 [The chameleon] keeps a vigil eye over the sun at high-noon.
Could a mere mortal continue to survive staring at the sun?
30 When the travelers halt to alight, it takes pleasure
in their treading over the embers of the burning heat.
31 At the center of the fire that is blazing, there is a bar of pure gold
that cannot be melted down from the flames.
32 You imagine that [where there is] departure from one's faith
there is perched atop every branch of the desert a cross.

(Diwan #29: 38–40)

The poem, clearly reflecting the time the poet was contemplating his departure from Sicily, may be divided into three segments: lines 1–15 comprises a physical debate of sorts concerning whether to remain or leave; lines 16–26 describe the actual journey (*rahil*); and lines 27–32 describe (*wasf*) a chameleon in the desert.

The first segment reads like a gnomic introduction (*muqaddima hikamiyya*), in the fashion of neoclassical poets, and a common feature of Ibn Hamdis's verses. It is built on a binary of fertile ground (familiar, hospitable, comfortable) and the wasteland (unknown, hostile, rocky). As we will see throughout his diwan, this binary will serve as a signifier for Sicily as *homeland* and desert as *exile*. It collapses the favored tropes of the amatory preface, the crying over abandoned ruins, and the anguish of the cruel and unjust twists of fate.

The second segment reads closely to the liminal segment of the classical Arabic ode (*qasida*) where the poet departs on the mount of a 'desert ship,' i.e., crossing the sea, that replaces the customary she-camel. However, lines 17–20 return to the anticipated images of desert camels who march to the chants of the cameleer, and eventually suffer bleeding (from whiplashes) and thirst, having exhausted their storage of water, that reinforce the images of the long and arduous journey. Lines 22–26 shift the imagery from the emaciated camels to the hostile terrain with images of scorching heat and fire. Most interesting, the poet inserts a line (21) in which he questions the logic of his decision to depart recalling the beginning of the poem: 'has he made, he wonders, a mistake?' This segment ends with the image of the poet/traveler being stricken with fever.

The third and final segment of the poem conjures the image of a chameleon, the transition of which is smoothly made with the evocation of the sand grouse and a wolf who, unlike the poet, draw benefit in the burning sands. Imaging the spectrum of the animal world of the desert, Ibn Hamdis pairs the sand grouse, the weak and vulnerable prey, with the wolf, the powerful and voracious predator, who find solace in the waves of moisture caused by the profuse sweating of the feverous poet. Through this image of the death–life cycle of thirst and quenching emerges the chameleon, a highly adaptable reptile best known for its ability to change its colors to blend in or camouflage itself against any environment. Ibn Hamdis's chameleon is not affected by the sun's burning rays and scorching heat, and it is able to survive what most men and beasts cannot.

In contrast to the earlier poem of the vermin in which we read an artistic personification of fleas, gnats, and bedbugs that assume the roles of drinking partners (*nudama'*) in a nightly ritual of celebration (*samar*) by feasting on the flesh and blood of the poet, here we see a process of 'animal-becoming' whereby the poet transforms himself into a Kafkaesque image of the chameleon who [will] survive the travails of a long and arduous desert-crossing into the unknown. Like Kafka's metamorphosis, Ibn Hamdis's transformation is a process of de-territorialization that allows him to separate from the beloved, i.e., his homeland Sicily, and not a young maiden of adolescent infatuation. It is not a *permanent* refuge but a *temporary* escape route from the current realities of a divided and soon-to-be defeated homeland.

The ambiguity of temporality and permanence, rooted in the debate of the first segment, is subtly but poignantly expressed in the pairing of the noun ***'ud*** with the adjective ***salib*** that appears first in line 14 and reappears at the end of the poem in line 32. ***'Ud*** has a primary meaning of 'a piece of wood,' a 'branch' or a 'twig.' It also carries the meaning of the musical 'lute'; it is etymologically connected to ***'awd***, being the verbal noun for 'return, returning,' and can be applied to an old road or an old camel. It also bears the meaning of 'custom' or 'habit.' ***Salib*** denotes 'solid' or 'sturdy,' and connotes the qualities of 'stubborn' or 'incalcitrant.' It also has a secondary meaning of 'cross' and/or a branding iron used for camels. The adjective-noun combination ***'salib al-'ud*** refers to someone who is robust of physique, and the noun construct ***'sulb al-'ud*** (robustness of physique) also refers to an aromatic plant-like substance with which one fumigates against noxious odors.

> He added a fifth to his coming, determination, nocturnal travel, and camels,
> being a piece of wood (*'ud*), for him the most difficult (*salib*) of all.
> You would think that [where there is departure] from one's faith
> there is perched atop every branch (*'ud*) of the desert a cross (*salib*).

In both lines the jumbling of the multiple meanings for both noun and adjective convey mixed messages and ambivalent emotions. The insertion of 'determination' (*'azm*), a poetic trope, a valued quality in the Arabian value system, and Ibn Hamdis's most conspicuous weapon of defense in his lifelong exile and his struggle to bring his homeland back into the Islamic fold, implies the hope of return he will harbor to his last, dying breath. In the last line of the poem, the idea of abandoning one's faith, and here by extension, his homeland, raises the ominous specter of the cross, the Christian crucifix (*salib*) that will, in his prescience, prevent his return. This combination of losing a homeland and the uncompromising resolve to return it to Islam is the mantra that will reverberate during his long life and be inscribed throughout his diwan.

3

THE FIRST DESERT CROSSING

Having made the difficult decision to depart from Sicily, Ibn Hamdis set out in 1078 to settle his family in their ancestral hometown of Sfax. By all accounts his stay there would not be a long one. With a saddlebag packed with mixed emotions, he embarked on this, his first journey, not only with the goal to reconnect to his ancestral roots but, more significantly, to begin his life-long quest to become a famous court poet. If he harbored any illusions of dismounting on a land depleted of Muslim divisiveness, he would soon be rudely awakened to an Ifriqiya that was as much, if not more, a hotly contested territory as his native Sicily. First, there was what still stood of the former Fatimid-supported Zirid dynasty, struggling with their newly acquired autonomy to expand their territories over tribal strongholds to carve out new areas of influence, and fighting off a persistent and pervasive Kharijite resistance that festered in large swathes of areas bordering on their strongholds of Sousse and Mahdia. The Kharijites constituted a sect of Islam that rejected both Sunni and Shi'ite claims to political rulership. They found fertile ground in the Maghreb, especially among the Berber populations who were often treated as 'second-class' citizens by the Arab elite. Second, there were the invasions of the Arabian Banu (Bani) Hilal and Banu Sulaym tribes (of whom more will be said) who, by the time of Ibn Hamdis's arrival, had made deep inroads into the internal politics of the central Maghreb. Compounding these were the intra-tribal squabbles among the Berber tribes as well as a resurgence of a Sunni Maliki *'ulama'* and their doctrinal and populist backlash against Fatimid Shi'ism.

IFRIQIYA: A DIVIDED AND TURBULENT MOTHERLAND

The Sfax that welcomed Ibn Hamdis and his family was ruled by Hamu ibn Malil al-Barghawati (r. 1059–1099), a scion of the tribe of Barghawata of the Masmoudi Berber confederation. The Barghawata make their earliest appearance in the Arabic historical archive as a tribe from the central Atlas region of the western Maghreb. They were instrumental in the Kharijite revolts in the middle of the eighth century, and their austere and eccentric mixture of Islamic beliefs and practices led to accusations against them of being infidels. Their relentless resistance to the rise of the Berber Almoravids (*al-Murabitun*) in 1059 and later the Almohads (*al-Muwahhidun*) in 1147 would eventually blunt their military and commercial muscle, and deflate the exuberance of their popularist religious and political acts of resistance.

In 1059, roughly twenty years prior to Ibn Hamdis's arrival in Sfax, the Zirid prince, al-Mu'izz ibn Badis, appointed one of his senior military commanders, Mansur al-Barghawati, as his regional governor to Sfax. Highly ambitious for power, and possibly sensing the vulnerable position the Zirids were forced into, Mansur severed his loyalties to his patron and decided to enter the city as its independent governor. In order to succeed, he took the bold step of establishing alliances with Arab tribes who had pitched tent on the outskirts of Sfax and in adjacent areas. Before he was able to launch his assault on the city and seize control, his equally ambitious cousin, Hamu ibn Malil al-Barghawati, arranged his assassination while he was bathing, and with poignant irony, in the *Sultan's Hammam*. The saga of intra-Muslim conflict that marked the period of Ibn Hamdis's birth continued with this murderous spectacle of violence, not just at the tribal level, but at the familial level as well. There was on the brighter side one life-affirming event, in the birth of Ibn Hamdis's second son, 'Umar, shortly after the family arrived in Sfax. Both his and his sister's immediate families found themselves once again inhabiting the same household headed by his beloved paternal aunt.

THE ZIRID DYNASTY OF IFRIQIYA

The Banu Ziri (the Zirids) were an extended clan of the Sanhaja Berber confederation and the first Berber dynasty to rule an independent 'state' in North Africa that began in 972 and ended in 1148 when the last Zirid prince, al-Hasan ibn 'Ali (r. 1121–1148), capitulated to an invading Norman Sicilian fleet under the command of Admiral George of Antioch. In 969, the fourth Fatimid caliph, al-Mu'izz li-din Allah (r. 953–975), having completed his campaigns and ultimate conquest of Egypt under the command of his brilliant general, Jawhar al-Siqilli, transferred the seat of his government to the newly established imperial city of Cairo (*al-Qahira*). Upon his departure he divided his North African realm into separate provinces, granting to Buluggin ibn Ziri (r. 972–983) the governorship of Ifriqiya, its most important region, politically, economically, and culturally. The Zirids had been loyal supporters of the Fatimid mission from the beginning and they served as a bulwark against the anti-Fatimid Zanata Berbers who also happened to be allies of the [Sunni] Ummayad caliphs of Cordoba, hostile rivals to the [Shi'ite] Fatimids. The Zirid militias were also highly instrumental in repelling the anti-Fatimid revolts spearheaded by Kharijite firebrand Abu Yazid Mukhallad ibn Kayrad (d. 947), notoriously known as 'the Donkey Man' (*Sahib al-himar*), whose mission succeeded in blockading Kairouan and holding it for a considerable period of time before its liberation.

The life of Ibn Hamdis spanned the reigns of the last five Zirid princes. His birth (1055) occurred during the reign of al-Mu'izz ibn Badis and he died (1133) during the reign of al-Hasan ibn 'Ali. With the exception of al-Mu'izz, whose death took place when Ibn Hamdis was still a young boy in Syracuse, the poet would compose in his professional career literally dozens of panegyric poems to all of them, especially to Yahya ibn Tamim (r. 1107–1116) and 'Ali ibn Yahya (1116–1121), who, as we shall see, launched numerous campaigns against the Normans in Sicily.

It was a cruel twist of fate for the young 'Abd al-Jabbar not to have lived through or have had a fully developed political consciousness of the forty-five-year-long transformative reign of the Zirid prince al-Mu'izz. If his later verses of political angst are any indication, Ibn Hamdis would most assuredly have approved of his responses to the political challenges of the times. When al-Mu'izz assumed the reins of power following the death of his father, Badis ibn Mansur (r. 995–1016), the Fatimid caliphate was securely ensconced in Egypt with its eyes veering more and more toward points East, leaving the affairs of governance in their former central Maghreb realm in the hands of its proxies. Finding himself in a position of strength, ruling vast areas of territory and presiding over a robust economy, the Zirid al-Mu'izz decided to change direction.

First, he consolidated his power both by land and sea, aiming to expand Zirid military and commercial influence in the central Mediterranean Basin. He made alliances with the Arab tribes in an attempt to push back his cousins and rivals, the Hammadids, who declared their independent state to the west in 1018 (and on whom more will be said in a later chapter). He also expended resources to push back against the increasing might and aggression of Muslim Sicily's Christian neighbors on the Italian mainland and across the Mediterranean. To this end, he resumed Ifriqiya's direct involvement in the affairs of the Muslims of Sicily. In 1025, he dispatched a massive flotilla to Sicily to negotiate among warring factions, but as fate would have it, much of the fleet sank in a storm at sea. Again, in 1029 he sent his son 'Abdallah back to Sicily in an attempt to repel early Norman forays into Sicily. Although this expedition failed to achieve its mission, and ended with significant numbers of Sicily's Muslim elite choosing to return with it to Ifriqiya as émigrés, as was mentioned above, it did succeed in raising the hopes of the island's Muslims in the specter of 'revived' North African saviors, a sentiment that would run continuously throughout Ibn Hamdis's later panegyrics.

Second, and in what should be viewed as a strong declaration of independence from the Shi'ite Fatimids of Egypt, al-Mu'izz declared allegiance to the Sunni 'Abbasid caliphate in Baghdad. By doing this he denounced Shi'ism and embraced the return of Sunni Islam as the sole legitimate 'religion of state,' an action that gained the ultimate political benefit of consolidating the power and influence of the Ifriqiyan

Maliki *'ulama'* who, in reality, never lost their powerful control over wide swathes of a disenfranchised urban and rural populace.

THE 'ARABS' OF ELEVENTH-CENTURY IFRIQIYA

The long reign of al-Mu'izz faced its greatest challenge in the onslaught of the Banu Hilal and Banu Sulaym tribes into the cities and countryside of the central Maghreb. The long-held accepted narrative is that these tribes, who had emigrated from the Arabian Peninsula in times of massive drought and settled first in Upper Egypt, were unleashed as an act of Fatimid revenge against the Zirids for their treasonous recognition of the 'Abbasid caliphate in Baghdad with promises to the invading tribes of power and riches in the central Maghreb. Their destruction of Kairouan wreaked havoc on the Zirid government, leaving historians, medieval and modern, to denounce them as a major destructive force in North African history. Famed fourteenth-century historian and social theorist Ibn Khaldun (1332–1406) was arguably the first and most explicit critic of these tribes, attributing to them massive urban and agricultural destruction of much of Maghrebi terrain. His writings would have significant influence on nineteenth-century French colonial *declensionist* theories that promoted the idea that the presence of Arabs and Islam in North Africa transformed the once 'granary of the Roman Empire' into a desolate wasteland.

Ibn Hamdis's views of the Arabs, who fare prominently as both real and imagined characters throughout his diwan, differed sharply. But who exactly were the *Arabs* of his extolling verses?

As a youth and a young man, passionate about classical Arabic poetry and aspiring to pursue a profession as a court poet, Ibn Hamdis was suckled on the Arabian ode (*qasida*), of both the *jahili* and post-Islamic (Umayyad and 'Abbasid) eras. Undoubtedly, his *Arabs* were the Arabs of the poetic canons, the poet-warrior-lovers of the pre-Islamic odes, whose military, political, and amorous adventures would provide the models and references to his own artistic creativity. Whether through reading texts or being exposed to the passing down of centuries of oral transmission, the lives and verses of these classical poets would serve as the linguistic and literary models to be emulated. Ibn Hamdis drew heavily from the language, imagery, stock phrases, as well as themes, tropes, and values inscribed in this rich Arabian literary tradition, as seen through the abundance of intertextuality in his diwan. The themes of *hasab wa nasab* (the sum total of qualities of honorableness combined with noble breeding), *ijara wa diyafa* (protection combined with hospitality), *muru'a* (manliness), *hilm* (forbearance), *shaja'a* (bravery), *jud*, *karam* (generosity), *'adl* (justice), and especially *'azm* (determination, resolve) would come to serve Ibn Hamdis in his quest to establish his reputation as a poet of rank and merit, as well as in developing his talents and skills in reworking classical themes to reflect his own times and give voice to his own personal values and goals. The *jahili* notion of the 'twists of fate,' as well as the post-Islamic views of God's divine will, are masterfully negotiated in ways that express the political and personal ups and downs of his long and turbulent life. Also, the tripartite structure of the Arabian ode, beginning with the amatory preface (*nasib*), to the departure (*rahil*), and ending with the boast (*fakhr*) provide a roadmap to much of his poetry by which he documented, with much credence and lyricism, his life experiences, such as lost love, lost homeland, and life on the road[s] of exile. It will be, as we will see again repeatedly, the medial segment (*gharad*) of the classical tripartite ode, the *rahil*, where Ibn Hamdis would remain tightly tethered to the classical Arabian poetic tradition. He would live to reach eighty years and his life's trajectory would be punctuated by many departures and many desert crossings. The *rahil*, with all of its stock tropes of hostile terrain, dangerous mountain passages, drought, emaciated camels and horses, encounters with the enemy, and strategies for survival in times and places of duress, came to provide him with all the familiar language and poetics to articulate both the public and private details of his life.

One could also imagine the *Arabs* of Ibn Hamdis as synonymous with the Arabs of the ninth-century Iraqi Arab polymath, al-Jahiz (776–868), that is, those dwellers of the desert, removed from and unaffected by the decadent and cosmopolitan ways of urban life, and who were the stubborn preservers of the classical Arabic language and values. Ibn Hamdis's lifelong commitment to what would be termed in modern parlance as 'pan-Arabism,' is informed by the ethos of preserving and extolling one's unadulterated genealogy (*nasab*) and identity, especially through language.

Third, one might consider the Hamdisian *Arabs* as the bedouins of Ibn Khaldun's binary of *Badu* (nomadic) and *Hadar* (sedentary). In fact, the terms '*arab*' and '*badu*' are often used interchangeably through the diwan. In contrast to his native homeland where the poet was born and raised close to the port of Syracuse and amid the greenery of Noto's meadows and forests, and where town and countryside were populated with merchants, artisans, and craftsmen, in close proximity to farmers and shepherds of the nearby fields and orchards, the topography of Ifriqiya was marked by clearer delineations between urban centers and farmlands, and surrounded by vast stretches of mountainous and flat desert expanses. Most likely by the time of Ibn Hamdis's arrival to his ancestral homeland of Sfax, the landscape of Bedouins was no longer that of the pre-Islamic Arabs of the Arabian Peninsula, but one still inhabited by communities of tribal families and confederations, Arabs and Berbers, who roamed the deserts and plains, living on the outskirts not far from the cities, villages, and settlements tangentially connected to marketplaces and neighborhoods of the urban centers.

And last, one must consider that the *Arabs* of Ibn Hamdis's verses were often the more proximate and politically more significant Banu Hilal and Banu Sulaym tribes who since 1048 began to conquer and occupy their own spaces in the vast stretches along the wider Maghreb. Contrary to the stark images of a marauding and destructive invasion by these Arabian tribes, projected as early as Ibn Khaldun in the fourteenth century, and embraced by European Orientalists in the nineteenth century, as mentioned above, we could read these Arabs as shrewd and powerful players in the power dynamics of the time. After all, it was the support of these tribesmen who helped Hamu wrest power away from his cousin in order to establish his own realm in Sfax. Thus, a picture of these tribesmen cleverly muscling their way into the military and political fabric of the Maghreb was in clear view of the highly astute and observant Ibn Hamdis whose task it was, as a court poet, to monitor these events and the characters who helped shape them. Another example will follow when, as will shall see in a later chapter, Ibn Hamdis composed a poem on the occasion of an unexpected Muslim victory over the army of Roger II, where he extols, in the combined stock phrases and imagery of *jahili* and Islamic poetics, the bravery and resolve of [these] *Arab* tribesmen in the defeat of the Norman Sicilian army at an old fortress on a tiny island off the coast of Tunisia.

ON THE DESERT HIGHWAY: TRAVELING WITH ARAB COMPANIONS

Ibn Hamdis composed a qasida, seemingly in his mature years, that was labeled in his diwan as "Remembering *Arab* Traveling Companions and Praising Compatriots of Syracuse." In it, the poet looks back and recalls a journey he took in his younger days through the desert of Ifriqiya in the company of *Bedouin* tribesmen. The assumption can soundly be made that this journey occurred at the end of his short stay in Sfax, and on his way westward along the North African littoral and heading toward al-Andalus. The poem, cited below in full translation, consists of forty-eight lines with interlacing motifs and formal structures that featured prominently in the classical Arabic ode. The ethos of the poem spans the pre-Islamic with the Islamic. Ibn Hamdis deftly juxtaposes *jahili* supernatural qualities of the desert warrior in all their celestial imagery, i.e., speaking swords, flying horses, and defying fate, with Islamic references. Beginning with line 11, the poet interjects the rhetorical prayer (*du'a'*) with a plea to God to moisten what was once fertile land, followed by several Quranic-laced verses as he narrates a battle with the infidel. The familiar qualities of noble breeding, honor, bravery, steadfastness, generosity, and protection, the core values of pre-Islamic panegyrics that carried over into Islam, provide a subtle poetic cohesion to the poem. The shift to the first person in line 10, "I've had the pleasure of their company in the most hostile terrain," brings the poet directly into the 'story' of the journey as both eye-witness and participant, allowing him the autobiographical space to localize (battling the Christians) and personalize (longing to return to his homeland) both the descriptions and events, real or imagined, of his recollections:

1 The blades of the white [swords] whose blossoms are drops of blood
graze on their white [helmets] which set the meadows abloom.
2 Giants in war, led by their stallions into battle,
[they tower high] above all that the raised swords cut down.
3 They descend onto the frontlines of attack like falling stars,
making clouds of rising dust and downpours of blood.
4 [Even] the lions would run from their thickets in fear,
whenever they dismount to pasture or to pitch tent.
5 Whenever they set out you see the twinkling of their lances
in the darkness of the clouds [they raise].
6 On the morning of battle, they are eloquent, strengthened by silence,
as the tongues [swords] of their sheathes do the talking for them.
7 It is as though their resolutions, if they could be embodied,
were [firmly held] hands when they smite necks.
8 Whenever the work of Fate and their work come face to face in combat,
with regard to the spirit of war heroes they are their true selves.
9 Bedouins, noble and pure of stock, bred among the finest breeds,
spur to battle hard-hoofed horses and camel steeds.
10 I've had the pleasure of their company in the most hostile terrain,
a wasteland where wolves howl and gazelles bleat.
11 May God water a sweet-teared spring [eye] that cried in lament
over its fertile lands that had a heart infatuated with it.
12 It was a land where the shining stars when they came out at night
welcomed me, while the land slept beneath them;
13 a land, where joy erases all grief from you,
and the good life wipes away all blemishes of misery.
14 How many a helpful, trusting comrade did I have there,
seeking not his own gain, but the honor to be generous,

15 pouring forth abundantly into the hand of a brother in need,
even though he himself was burning with distress.
16 If the heroes retreated, he would attack,
and his sword would release with his right hand the blood of the lawless infidel.
17 Because of him a great army, like the sea, stirs;
its waves are his armor, whose coat of mail he fortifies.
18 We are the people of the frontier (*thaghr*) whose teeth (*thughur*) smile at war
whenever war makes its menacing face.
19 Our young are suckled on the milk of the jugular vein,
weaned at war's apron strings.
20 We stand at the buttocks [rear lines] and breast [front lines]
of the battlefield, while spears bounce off our chests.
21 If knights are counted, we number twofold,
one valiant soldier among us almost equals an army.
22 We are placed at the end to attack as part of each rearguard;
the rear position of what faces all kinds of death is [actually] a front position.
23 If a protracted war comes to rely on us,
it will not pelt [us] with shooting stars. [Quran 67:5; 105:3–4]
24 From the weave of our horses, war weaves on the day of battle
a mantle over us, with our horses as their stripes.
25 Hovering above in pursuit of every valiant soldier mounted on a stallion,
the vultures of war swoop down, ready to devour [the dead].
26 And many a swift horse, carrying a courageous warrior,
is conceded its superiority over the swift bolt of lightning.
27 We launched an attack on the enemies of God in their own abode,
in a ship that was submerged into death's abyss.
28 It floated around the infidels and made for us a protective shield
against them, like birds hovering in a circle in the sky.
29 [It was as though it were] a camel pregnant without its stallion,
brought to its knees by disaster when it gave birth on the shores of the Rum.
30 Akin to war, and erected for its cause,
these ships, filled with lions (asad), floated on the water.*
[* Perhaps an allusion to Asad (lion) Ibn al-Furat,
Muslim conqueror of Sicily.]

31 As though the bows, set at the rear of the ships,
had their arrows fly high as if they were coming from the front.
32 They eject fuel that rides the waters and burns like molten lead,
like that with which hell burns the faces [of the disbelievers].
[Quran 18:29]
33 Huge ships (*mada'in*) launch attacks on the cities (*mada'in*) of the infidels;
they conquer them by the sword, and they plunder.
34 Although the enemy donned the protective shield of the blade,
their heroes shirked in war, and they [believers] attacked.
35 It was like a mirage in which they plunged onto flat, open land,
and the shimmering of armor looked like the eyes of locusts watching them.
36 Like noblemen, we waited patiently for them to submit,
[as they were still] unable to taste the sweetness [of victory] before swallowing the bitterness [of war].
37 Our attack left its boned meat in their mouths;
their molars, once sharp swords, were now blunted.
38 The iron [sword] that remained in our hands was our spokesman;
when in someone else's hands it would have been mute.
39 The wings of our banners were flapping in the wind above us,
as though the blood of the heroes was red dye splattered over them.
40 Thus a flash of lightning lit up from the direction of Abra* in the homeland,
like a nimble hand which greets with the fingertips.
[* Ancient Near Eastern city located in the eastern Arabian Peninsula.]
41 The lightning made the tear ducts gush forth from sleepless eyes
and soothed them with light when the night was dark.
42 Oh, what a wonder a visit whose phantom visited their eyes,
in which, out of drowsiness, there was delusion.
43 The phantom weakened my feet as I stopped at the traces,
whenever it is moistened, it is struck.
44 A vast land and its bounty has sent me the sweetness of its fragrance,
without which I would have plunged into distress.
45 Beyond the darkness, there is the light of morning;
like a black horse covered with foamy sweat on its chest after a long gallop.

46 I long for my lands in whose earth
rest in peace the bones and joints [remains] of my people,
47 Just like a strong camel, led astray in the dark of night,
moaning with longing to return to its homeland.
48 The full bloom of youth has wilted in my hands,
but my mouth still mutters the memory of my youth.
(Diwan #269: 412–416)

The poem's use of 'Arab' and 'Bedouin' brings back once again the question of who are the collective *'Arab* of Ibn Hamdis's diwan. There are references in this poem that suggest it was composed at a later point in his life. Also, given the tender age of mid-twenties when the poet departed from his beloved Syracuse, and the fact that he spent less than a year in Sfax before embarking on this journey, it would seem unlikely that he lived or experienced directly at that time the firepower and swashbuckling of warfare he so deftly described in this poem. The beauty of the poem lies in its mediation between the recollections of a young man nurtured on reading vast amounts of Arabic poetry imbued with the valor and bravado of warriors and lovers, and between the lived experiences of an impressionable young man navigating his way between losing a homeland and embarking on a career aiming for fame and fortune.

The Arabs as 'traveling companions' may be read as much the heroes of classical poetry as they are the Bedouins, and most likely the Arabian tribesmen of the Banu Hilal, who crossed the deserts as sheepherders, cameleers, merchants, or even guns-for-hire in these turbulent times.

In light of the several verses throughout the poem in which Ibn Hamdis conjures various images of the infidel, i.e., enemies of God (line 27), the infidels (line 33), and more ungently, the *Rum* (read: the invading Normans in Sicily: line 29), we may read the Hamdisian *Arab/ Bedouin* as more than poetic (fictional) heroes. In them Ibn Hamdis sees the possibilities of a new line of offense against the invaders and soon-to-be occupiers of his homeland.

The last seven lines of the poem illustrate what will be a hallmark of Ibn Hamdis's poetry: the nexus of literary artistry and a political poetics steeped in a highly personalized lyricism that draws in all Arab, Islamic, and Sicilian identities. These closing seven lines commence with the image of the pre-Islam phantom of the beloved (*tayf*) who appears over the abandoned ruins (*atlal*) of a former abode (Sicily), continue with the black horse 'foaming sweat after a long gallop' (*rahil*), and end with the poet's projection of himself (*fakhr*) as a 'sturdy camel' who is 'longing to return to its homeland.' Like the chameleon of the earlier poem who survives the hardships of the desert, Ibn Hamdis employs "becoming animal" to envision himself as the camel who will spend its life seeking to return home by keeping it in his memory ("but my mouth still utters the memory of my youth").

Ibn Hamdis's departure from Sfax was especially difficult given that it amounted to abandoning his young family in an unstable place and time, but also because he was venturing into the unknown. Until his dying breath, the poet would express the anguish of feeling guilt and neglect for being an absentee husband, father, nephew, and cousin. But the call to glory was powerful, and he answered it unflinchingly. Contrary to what modern scholars, both Arab and Italian, have posited, that Ibn Hamdis left Sicily and, by extension, left Sfax to join the Muslim armies to battle (jihad) against the Christian reconquest, Ibn Hamdis embarked on his first major *rahil* as an aspiring poet. Had religious fervor or the desire to fight to save his homeland been his foremost concern, he would never have left Sicily where the enemy had entered, battle lines were being drawn, and the urgency to fight and defend was most powerful.

However, mastery of 'academic' classical Arabic poetry as a discipline of Arabic philology was not enough. In the time and place of his lifespan, an aspiring poet needed a patron, a court, an audience, and rival poets with whom he could hone his skills and refine his craft. Neither a politically divided Muslim Sicily living under the dark clouds of a full-scale Norman invasion, nor a destabilized and fractured Ifriqiya could provide him with a suitable environment where he could grow as a famous court poet. Heeding a call that we could easily describe as 'Go West, young man!' Ibn Hamdis's embarked on his journey 'in the company of Bedouins' that would bring him to the gates of Seville.

4

LA DOLCE VITA IN SEVILLE

On a dark and sultry late summer evening in the year 1078, a disheartened Ibn Hamdis sat in his quarters of a travelers' inn on the outskirts of the city of Seville, situated in the lower reaches of the Guadalqivir River, pondering his fate and his future. He arrived after what must have been a long and grueling journey, having traversed the wide expanses and winding mountain passages of the North African desert, only to face the short but treacherous crossing through the narrow Strait that bridges the African coast to the Iberian Peninsula. His hope was to join the court of al-Mu'tamid ibn 'Abbad, king and ruler of the petty kingdom of Seville, as a court poet. The scorching sun of the day had already set, and the wind blew such that the rustling of the leaves of the almond trees and orange groves that surrounded the inn intermingled with his thoughts. Having failed thus far to secure an audience with the king, Ibn Hamdis made once again the difficult decision to depart.

But fate, this time, would work in his favor. While packing his bags in preparation for his journey back to Ifriqiya, he heard a voice from a distance calling out his name. He looked out from a lone small window in his room and caught sight of a young page approaching the inn, carrying a rein tied to a horse in one hand, and a lantern in the other. A stunned and curious Ibn Hamdis went down and greeted the page. He came to inform the guest that al-Mu'tamid had agreed to grant him an audience, and that he must return immediately with the page to the palace. When they arrived, the page escorted the young traveling poet to the king's quarters. After greetings of welcome, al-Mu'tamid instructed Ibn Hamdis to take a seat. Several moments passed before the king headed toward a window in his chamber and looked out, and then summoned his guest to come and stand beside him. On the far end of the courtyard that lay beneath the king's chamber stood an ironsmith's furnace that had two glass doors a servant woman was opening and closing to stoke the flames. All of a sudden, the king improvised the first hemistich of a line of poetry describing the fire and challenged Ibn Hamdis to complete it with the same meter and rhyme, matching it or besting it. After several rounds of poetic sparring, al-Mu'tamid was sufficiently impressed and invited the young Sicilian to join his royal retinue.

This brief but telling anecdote was recorded in Ibn Hamdis's diwan (Diwan #344: 543), in the form of introductory epigram describing the poem's occasion. Its value lies not only in its insight into the world of court poets and poetry but also, and for our intended purposes here, in its dismissal of any notion that Ibn Hamdis was a *mujahid* who traveled to al-Andalus to join a jihad against the Christian Reconquest. Above all, it draws attention to the power and advantages of patronage at this time and place of Arab-Islamic civilization, as well as the role that poetry continued to play in court circles and in public [read: political] life.

THE 'ABBADID KINGDOM OF SEVILLE

Muhammad ibn 'Abbad al-Mu'tamid bi-allah (r. 1069–1095) was the third and last member of the 'Abbadid dynasty that reigned over the southwest of al-Andalus throughout most of the eleventh century. The dynasty came into existence following the demise of the Cordoban caliphate (929–1030) and the dismemberment of Muslim Spain into breakaway kingdoms and principalities ruled by individuals who have come to be referred to as the 'Petty Kings' or 'Party Kings' (*muluk al-tawa'if*). The 'Abbadid family traced its origins to the ancient Arabian tribe of the Banu Lakhm, and it ranked among one of the most prestigious subgroups of the powerful Arab elite who, as military conquerors, ascended to power in the Maghreb (North Africa, Spain, and Sicily) following the successes of the wars of conquest in the first

Islamic century. His grandfather, Abu al-Qasim Muhammd ibn ʿAbbad (r. 1023–1042), had served as a chief judge (*qadi*) of Seville before seizing power in the chaos that arose from the fall of the Ummayad caliphate of Cordoba in 1031.

It was his son, and al-Muʿtamid's father, ʿAbbad II al-Muʿtadid bi-allah (1042–1069) who brought might and muscle to the family's dynastic rule. In his nearly thirty-year reign, he succeeded in expanding the territories of his realm, fought off any serious threats from rival petty kings and princes, and promoted the cause of the Andalusian Arab high culture against the rising tides of the growing Berber populations and their increasing military and political strength. From a gruesome report that attests to his ferocious determination, we learn that ʿAbbad II invited a number of Berber warlords to his palace in Seville under the pretense of mending fences. While they were relaxing in a steam at the royal hammam, the story goes, he had all the doors and windows of the bathhouse bolted, leaving each and every one of them to perish by suffocation.

Upon the death in 1069 of his powerful and ruthless father, al-Muʿtamid acceded to the throne in Seville, and to his own credit, he succeeded in annexing the defeated but still important and highly revered city of Cordoba and its suburbs to his realm. He continued the expansive policies of his father, and at times he displayed similar impulses to murder enemies or disloyal members of his entourage. A case in point is the favored court poet, Ibn ʿAmmar, a charismatic and highly gifted *muwallad*, i.e., a descendant of converted Christians of al-Andalus, from Shilb (now Silves in southern Portugal), whom the new king appointed as his vizier (chief minister). Because of a foolish decision to seize power for himself after his successful military expedition to Murcia, the treasonous Ibn ʿAmmar was captured and strangled to death at the hands of his benefactor and trusted friend, al-Muʿtamid. Also, like his father, the new king was a patron of scholarship and culture, priding himself for presiding over one of the most illustrious courts in the Muslim west. It would be his grave misfortune, however, to rule at a time when the Christian conquest was enjoying something of a revival, especially in the persona of Alfonso VI, to whom we will return in the next chapter.

MUSLIM SPAIN AND MUSLIM SICILY: A COMPARATIVE VIEW

In the winter of 1184, the renowned Granadan traveler-scholar, Abu al-Husayn Muhammad Ibn Jubayr (1145–1217), landed at the port of Messina in the northeast corner of Sicily and disembarked with his fellow passengers from a damaged ship that had been battered by a storm at sea on its way back from the pilgrimage to Mecca. His sojourn on the island would last nearly a month, and he would eventually record in his diary the following observation:

> The prosperity of the island surpasses description. It is enough to say that it [Sicily] is a daughter of Spain in the extent of its cultivation, in the luxuriance of its harvests, and in its well-being, having an abundance of varied produce, and fruits of every kind and species.
>
> (*Travels*, translated by R. Broadhurst, 1907: 580 (339))

The pairing of Muslim Spain and Muslim Sicily is an academic enterprise that goes far back in time. There is much similarity in their histories, and equally as much that differentiated the one from the other. When Ibn Hamdis landed on Iberian soil after his arduous North African desert crossing he found himself on recognizable and hospitable terrain. As much as the Ifriqiyan landscape stimulated and enriched his romantic imaginings of Arabian Bedouin life and culture that brought an intimacy and added a 'touch of the real' to his study of classical Arabic poetry, the fertile ground and moist atmosphere of southern Spain awakened vivid recollections of his native Sicily. All of the lushness of the environment, the diversity of peoples, languages, and faiths, and even the bickering and infighting among his co-religionists, were all too familiar to him.

What had drawn Ibn Hamdis there most urgently was not, however, the physical landscape of al-Andalus but the rich and extensive terrain of royal court culture that was a venue for promoting scholarly and cultural creativity. In his new patron, al-Mu'tamid, Ibn Hamdis found a man, and the son of a man, whose physical and political strengths matched his intellectual and artistic sensitivities and aspirations. Both al-Mu'tamid and his father were poets themselves. Much of the 'Abbadid political success, as we have mentioned, was due to its broad appeal to Arabism, less in an ethnic or tribal sense, but more by way of following a long continuum of a shared language and a powerful and robust literary culture in which poetry stood out as one of its most cherished components.

The 'Abbadid Court of Seville prided itself on its self-conscious and deliberate imitation of the Cordoban caliphal court that reached full bloom when the third Umayyad emir, 'Abd al-Rahman III, who carried the agnomen of *al-Nasir li Din Allah* (The Victor of God's Religion), declared himself 'caliph' and his government as a 'caliphate' in 929. In the aftermath of its humiliating downfall in 1031, the 'Abbadids seized power and sought to construct their own court as a memory palace of its Umayyad predecessors. This entailed replicating courtly practices, such as summoning the best and brightest of religious and legal scholars, scientists, philosophers, men of letters, and poets to intercourse with the vast array of government employees, ministers, scribes, and accountants, to forge bonds and linkages that would be bound in loyalty through the generous patronage of the king.

The 'Abbadid Court in the reign of al-Mu'tamid, in all its attempts to revive the splendor and reach the heights of the Umayyad Court that thrived in the once glorious and unsurpassable city of Cordoba, was exactly what Ibn Hamdis was searching for. As a young Sicilian growing up in mid-eleventh-century Syracuse, he undoubtedly knew something about the power and prestige of a royal court. In addition to his knowledge and admiration of poets and poetry that were produced in the heyday of the 'Abbasid and Buyid Courts in Baghdad, as well as the Hamdanid Court in Aleppo, there was the more recent and proximate example of the Sicilian Kalbid Court that flourished in Palermo—even if only briefly—in the decades immediately preceding his birth. In imitation of both eastern Arab-Muslim and western Byzantine models of courtly culture and praxis, the Kalbids, having achieved a great deal of autonomy in Sicily once the Fatimids evacuated from the Maghreb and moved their capital to Cairo, gained much political and cultural capital from the coterie of court poets who extolled their royal patrons by manipulating and reworking the traditions of the classical Arabic panegyric, lavishing praise, deservedly or not, on their powerful patrons in exchange for fame and fortune.

There was another reason why Ibn Hamdis headed west. As the Kalbid dynasty was inflicting homicidal and suicidal wounds onto itself, the conditions and demands for a leisurely pastime of wine and poetry grew scarce. We saw that in 1025, and then 1029, the Zirid al-Mu'izz ibn Badis dispatched naval expeditions from Mahdia to Sicily in attempts to negotiate with the warring factions in Sicily. In 1029 came the first wave of emigration from the island: Muslims loyal to the Fatimid-Kalbid government, predominantly bureaucrats and military personnel, fled to resettle and serve in the Fatimid government in Cairo; Maliki jurists and religious scholars returned to Ifriqiya, recently purged by the Maliki 'ulama' of its Shi'ite jurists and other heterodox Muslim practitioners who had occupied major government-appointed positions ever since the Fatimids put an effective end to Aghlabid rule in 909; highly accomplished scholars of philosophy and philology headed to Baghdad and points east where the luminaries of the Islamic sciences hailed; and poets went to al-Andalus, mainly to Seville. Ibn Hamdis was following the traffic signs of exile in that direction.

The extant bio-bibliography of medieval Muslim Sicily has preserved several names of poets who fled the island and sought their sanctuary at the Andalusian courts: Sulayman ibn Muhammad al-Tarabanshi (from Trapani) first traveled to Ifriqiya and then settled in al-Andalus, proffering his poetic services to various petty princes; Abu Said 'Uthman ibn 'Atiq survives with four lines of a panegyric praising Mu'tasim ibn Samaduh of Almeria, a sometimes rival to al-Mu'tamid; Abu al-Hasan 'Ali ibn 'Abd al-Jabbar (a.k.a. Ibn al-Kammuni), is remembered for composing an elegy to Sicily while in Seville:

> Our abode, when we inhabited it,
> lived in the shade of a sweet and fertile life;
> Security wrapped its blanket over it, then its very mention
> departed with those who departed;
> And those who failed to give thanks for the blessings bestowed on them
> were given the bitter instead of the sweet.

And, perhaps, the most famous of these Sicilian poets in Seville was Mus'ab ibn Muhammad ibn Abi al-Furat al-Qurashi, better known as Abu al-'Arab who, being born in Palermo in 1034, was a generation older than Ibn Hamdis, and likely among the first to precede him to al-Mu'tamid's court. In the closing lines of a panegyric he composed to his new patron, he echoes fellow Sicilian exiles in lauding the protection and hospitality (*ijara wa diyafa*) of their Andalusian host:

> I was rescued and my life is renewed,
> for the safety of a young man after great fear brings new life.
> The days have done great and kindly deeds,
> such that my today and tomorrow compete for its kindness.

This small coterie of Sicilian poets who sought and received refuge at al-Mu'tamid's court was most assuredly outnumbered by a larger number of Andalusian poets, themselves fleeing from the rapidly increasing number of petty kingdoms and principalities throughout the Iberian peninsula that were falling to the Christian conquests. Perhaps the best example of these Andalusian poets is found in Ibn al-Labbana (d. 1113).

Abu Bakr Muhammad ibn 'Isa al-Dani (from the city of Denia) derived his nickname *Ibn al-Labbana*, and by which he is best known, from the fact that he was the son of a dairymaid. She was described as a woman of humble origins and modest means who, nonetheless, educated her sons and lived a highly moral life. Ibn al-Labbana enjoyed a close and affectionate relationship with al-Mu'tamid and, like Ibn Hamdis, he would be called upon to compose panegyrics to his patron on numerous occasions. Unlike Ibn Hamdis, he composed verses not only in the classical qasida tradition but also in the then current and fashionable genre of the *muwashshah*, a multi-lined strophic verse poem usually consisting of five stanzas, alternating with a refrain with a running rhyme. Also, unlike Ibn Hamdis, Ibn al-Labbana was a polymath who purportedly composed two major works on the 'Abbadids: *Siqt al-durar wa laqt al-Zahar* (The Hail of Pearls and the Plucking of Flowers), being a compilation of poems composed by the 'Abbadid princes; and *Nazm al-suluk fi mawa'iz al-muluk* (The Composition of Etiquette in the Sermons of Kings). Both works are now lost, but their existence draws attention to the author's much deeper personal, political, and scholarly ties to the 'Abbadid dynasty and its court culture.

Ibn Hamdis followed in their footsteps and joined their ranks. He spent thirteen years in Seville, perhaps the most productive and transformative period of his professional life, taking full advantage of an intellectual and cultural florescence that offered opportunities for social and artistic advancement. In contrast to the political chaos that marked his early years in Sicily, and unlike the backwater provincial climate of Sfax, where he nonetheless achieved the valuable experience and first-hand knowledge of Bedouin life and traditional Arab nomadic ways, he was thrown, in Seville, into a highly charged and fiercely competitive environment where kings, princes, ministers, soldiers, and merchants flaunted their mastery of the canons of classical Arabic poetry and tested their talents at composing innovative verses that reflected their own place and time. The elaborate and well-fortified palatine compound of the 'Abbadid kings and their vibrant court patronage provided an ideal atmosphere for scholarly and cultural activities hermetically sealed off from any political or social annoyances taking place beyond the gates of the royal premises. And, despite the wider political divides that separated Muslim Spain from Muslim Sicily throughout the Middle Ages, i.e., the animosity between the Umayyad emirate of Cordoba and the pro-'Abbasid emirate of the Aghlabid dynasty of Qayrawan in the ninth century, and the following century's bitter rivalries between the Andalusian Umayyad caliphate and the Ifriqiyan Fatimid caliphate, the cultural connections and literary affinities between Muslim Sicilians and Muslim Spaniards that were developed and fostered at the royal courts became a lived experience for Ibn Hamdis in Seville. This was best expressed by the twentieth-century Italian scholar of Arabic literature, Francesco Gabriele: "*I veri legami tra Spagna e Sicilia araba non appartengono dunque alla storia politica e militare, quando a quella della cività e della cultura*" (F. Gabrieli, "Arabi di Sicilia e Arabi di Spagna": 121).

ELEGY TO A FATHER

In the early years of Ibn Hamdis's life in Seville, the young poet, now surrounded by men of culture who shared his passion for poetry, was stunned by news of his father's death. In what would become his lifelong custom of fusing the personal with the professional, he composed an elegy to his father, the first of several elegies he would compose to family members, in which he intersects the past with the present, and homeland with exile.

1 The hand of fate both wounds and heals,
   your world destroys and is destroyed.
2 Your Lord inherits it owners
   and He revives their exhausted bones.
3 I have seen death wipe out humanity,
   and death's bite has no cure.
4 The hand of the perpetrator stretches out
   to the offspring of death, to our souls.
5 Every man's ears have seen
   the passing of nations that rise and fall.
6 The soul of every man is borrowed,
   and what is borrowed must be returned.
7 May God, by His mercy, water my father's grave
   with the clouds of dawn and eventide,
8 and make his spirit leave his body
   and go to the land of comfort and repose.
9 How much of pure disposition did he embody,
   as well as a sublime will to reach the heights!
10 First among nobility of the highest order,
   the light of day paled in his glory.
11 If only Time had his high moral standards,
   then its sources would indeed have purity.
12 His death was announced to me in a foreign land.
   How frightening it is to hear of such a calamity!
13 It has reddened my pure white tears,
   and turned to white my long black side curls.
14 It is as though living in a land of exile
   makes one forget the mentioning of the stranger.
15 I kept an image of him in my heart,
   and kept close to me his distant soil.
16 For this noble man I wailed like a bereaved mother,
   with only my verses to console.
17 Heir to a long line of excellence, a gentleman
   whose life's course was as high as the stars.

18 He passed on, having lived beyond the limits of forbearance.
So, who could move the immovable mountains?
19 I may forget all save the day of separation,
when the secrets in our eyes were revealed.
20 The time came for us to bid farewell
with our cheeks flushed with tears of pearl.
21 Here I stand barefoot over Time's embers
with the passing of my father.
22 And so we went; I, to a land of bitter exile,
and he, to a land of sweet repose.
23 His sound judgment lifted me to the level of the stars,
my guiding light their highest shimmer.
24 I have heard the good advice of my sheikh
whose land is now far away from me.
25 His wise words still ring in my ear,
as he wanted to tell me that life is but a journey.
26 He passed on having trod the glorious path,
in the footsteps of his father and his father's father,
27 noblemen who perished in the perilous twists of fate,
while they made their glorious feats survive in time.
28 He passed on having been my soul mate
with his noble spirit touching my sorrow,
29 and along with this sorrow from his death
our crying eyes flooded our cheeks.
30 I am one remaining in deep grief after him,
shedding tears of blood over him.
31 For hours on end I have cried for my father,
as the parched wastelands [of exile] witness my tears.
32 My blazing anguish has not been extinguished,
my tears have not dried up.
33 My soul as long as it continues to be
will meet the same fate as he.
(Diwan #330: 522–524; translation with Sheida Dayani)

As a young poet out to learn the ropes and prove his mastery of the canons of classical Arabic poetry, Ibn Hamdis clearly demonstrated his observance and faithfulness to the standards in composing a proper elegy (*ritha'*). He begins this poem with the familiar gnomic introduction in which he bemoans the cruel and fickle hand of fate, and man's powerlessness in standing up against it. Ibn Hamdis then transitions from this pre-Islamic world-view with an Islamic plea to God (*du'a'*), asking for His mercy on his father's soul through the image of watering his grave in which the deceased will rest in peace. The poem contains the customary announcement of death (*na'iy*), as well as the de rigueur verses of personal anguish (*tafajju'*) that include images of reddened tears and whitened side curls and, most importantly, a litany of the deceased's finest qualities. Both of these segments are amplified in their emotional force with the frequent reference to the poet's departure from his homeland and his loved ones, and in the loneliness of his exile in a foreign land.

SERVING THE PATRON: THE POLITICAL PANEGYRIC

As a newcomer to the 'Abbadid court where he was surrounded by other poets with comparable talents and skills, Ibn Hamdis needed to find his place, define his uniqueness, and make his mark amid a fiercely competitive environment. Since the panegyric was the poetic genre of artistic choice and professional necessity, given the poets' assignment to serve as royal propagandists, Ibn Hamdis wasted little time in showcasing his skills in this regard. In the following poem, composed soon after he settled in court, and not long after the news of his father's death had arrived from Sicily, the poet chose to forego the customary gnomic introduction. The occasion, i.e., singing the praises of his new patron, had no call for brooding over ill fortune or pessimism. The opening line commences directly with praise to the king, and by referring to God he implies divine approval of his right to rule, a theme that will run throughout the poem. In keeping with tradition, Ibn Hamdis structures his verses that include the gamut of the essential attributes that define a righteous ruler: physical beauty, physical strength, military prowess, sound judgment, courage, generosity, and 'protection combined with hospitality' (*ijara wa diyafa*):

1 Your countenance has removed all inflammation from our eyes;
and in your sight God has brought forth all that was distant.
2 In your reflection the thoroughbred carries itself in four images:
the full moon; the lofty peak; the deep blue sea; and the mighty lion.
3 The human eye gleams shiny black when it catches sight of you,
[a sight] that chases away all worry and grief.
4 All are delighted by a face in whose features glows a light
that makes a true believer even more devout.
5 Your sword has been distinguished for its defense of the righteous faith;
and you remain always distinguished by your incomparable generosity.
6 You are imagined as a lion endowed with swords for claws,
and your coat of mail is reckoned to be thick skin and a mane,
7 as though [this lion] has sheathes in war that come forth to drink blood
in the tradition of the [mighty] Hindi sword.
8 Because of the sheer courage in your right hand [alone],
your smite becomes all the fiercer when drunk on blood.
9 On the day of battle your spear is raised,
and it chomps on the livers of lions.
10 Our religion derives strength (*mu'tamid*) from a king who spends his waking hours
drawing strength (*mu'tamad*) from the Most Compassionate.
11 It is as though there were shooting stars counted among [this king's] spears,
with which he destroys all the tyrants of infidelity who come forth.
12 Whenever he raises the banner of war in full resolve,
his hands untie every complexity with his judgements.
13 Vigorous and steadfast, whenever any worthy rival comes to contest him,
you imagine it to be the [great] battle of Uhud.*
[* Uhud is the mountain site of an early battle waged by the Meccans in revenge for their defeat at Badr that ended in a Muslim defeat due to poor planning and coordination.]
14 Pure thoroughbreds, with valiant knights of fury advancing,
like female demons bearing lions on their backs.

15 Whenever a sky clouds up with billows of battle dust,
the Samhari swords stand erect like pillars for them.
16 Every courageous soldier is covered from head to toe in steel,
its coldness coagulates blood into foam [that rises] above him.
17 Rushing forth with a sharp lance with its tip aroused on the day of battle,
it brings sleep to the eyes of the sleepless.
18 [A king] who does not drink the sap of the body sheathed in chain mail
until he sees the tip of his sword devouring the flesh.
19 You make a river of blood flow from your enemies,
you leave purposely the land where they stood drenched in blood.
20 O you who rotate the cycle of generosity
and whose justice supports every man in need,
21 people of hope flock to you, and by your very mention
they inhale the aroma of musk and find in you a cure.
22 You never disappointed one hopeful of your magnanimity,
you never left a thirsty (*sadd*) man with nothing to quench his thirst.
(or: you never turned away a man in exile (*sadd*))
23 I now have no distance in my distant wandering from my homeland,
after it you have made Hims* a country for me.
[* One of the proverbial homelands of the ancient Arabs.]
24 As a substitute for my closest kin I was given its kin;
May God not separate me from them in all eternity.
25 How many of my people in a land far away the earth embraces,
I could not see any of them because of my distance.
26 The death of my father did not compel me to depart from your abode,
even though the death of a father may greatly distress the son.
27 You did not block my path to return to them;
you made my separation (*sifad*) from them a blessing (*safad*).
28 This most tender loving care, whose sweetness abounds in my heart,
cools off the scorching heat of [my] sorrow.

(Diwan #101: 170–171)

This powerful ode, a virtuoso display of all the rhetorical devices particular to the *badi'* movement of neo-classical poetry, is distinguished for its closing verses. From lines 23–28 the poet will insert his own—autobiographical—voice that provides concrete evidence to al-Mu'tamid's quality of 'protection with hospitality.' Here, Ibn Hamdis seizes the occasion to mention, or remind, his audience, including the subject of his panegyric, that he has been exiled far from his homeland and loved ones, and has recently suffered the death of his father. The poem ends with what Ibn Hamdis will attribute to al-Mu'tamid as being his finest quality: that he has rescued the stranger from his solitude, and offers him a sanctuary that 'cools off the scorching heat of [his] sorrow.' Thus, by identifying himself as Sicily's premier exile in the service of his patron, he established his mark of distinction.

COURT POET AS COURT FUNCTIONARY

Ibn Hamdis's role as court poet in Seville was not limited to artistic production. Like his peers elsewhere throughout the Muslim and Christian Middle Ages, he was not only expected to compose poems legitimating the patron's governance, but was often summoned to render non-literary services, be they diplomatic, political, and even military. A brief seven-line poem Ibn Hamdis composed as a reply to al-Mu'tamid's summons to him is a case in point. In 1085, the king commanded his vizier, the above-mentioned Ibn 'Ammar, to head an expedition to seize control of the principality of Murcia and annex it to Seville. Ibn 'Ammar had been a childhood friend of al-Mu'tamid, it should be recalled, and was appointed vizier when al-Mu'tamid ascended the throne. Ibn 'Ammar enjoyed a stellar reputation for his unusual intelligence, his masterful poetry, and his exceptional skills as a chess player. Upon the completion and success of his military mission, he requested that he be appointed governor of Murcia, to which the king acquiesced. Shortly thereafter, Ibn 'Ammar, acting on his impulses for power, declared his independence from his patron. Al-Mu'tamid responded quickly. He had Ibn 'Ammar arrested and brought back to Seville in chains and, as mentioned above, strangled him with his own two hands on the banks of the Guadaquivir. Ibn Hamdis, summoned to be a witness to this event, composed his poem (Diwan #71: 110–111) in which he joyously praised the king, boasted his obedience to the summons, and pledged his loyalty to him. The 'happy' tenor of the poem undoubtedly reflects a degree of gloating on Ibn Hamdis's part over the demise of a strong rival as court poet and competitor for the king's esteem and affections.

THE LOOMING THREAT OF THE CHRISTIAN RECONQUEST

The poem cited above was composed in a difficult period for not only the 'Abbadid dynasty in Seville, but for what remained of Islam on the Iberian Peninsula. On the one hand, Ibn 'Ammar's disloyalty and grab for power were, by now, all too familiar actions that tore at the fabric of Muslim unity. What Ibn Hamdis had known, or heard about at a distance, as a young boy in Syracuse about the bitter divides among the three warlords of Sicily that facilitated the Norman Conquest, and what he witnessed first-hand about the violent infighting among the Barghawatas of Sfax, not to mention the threats to the Zirid princes from the invading Arab and rival Berber tribes throughout Ifriqiya, were now appearing in Ibn Hamdis's full view close and up front as he navigated his way through the palatial corridors and battlefields of al-Mu'tamid's Court. We see that a number of his panegyrics were composed and delivered—to court audiences and beyond—on occasions when the king returned from a battle fought against Muslim rivals. There are, however, other panegyrics Ibn Hamdis composed to celebrate his patron on occasions when the victory was against the armies of the Christian conquest, especially of those commanded by Alfonso VI. Suffice to say that the later decades of the eleventh century, that is, the period when Ibn Hamdis departed from Sicily and spent his years at the 'Abbadid Court in Seville, witnessed an upward turn for Iberian Christians as they sought to conquer territory long held by the Muslims. The fall of the mighty Cordoban emirate in 1031, and the subsequent rise of petty kingdoms in its immediate aftermath, it should be recalled, would come to a decisive moment with the conquest (more of a capitulation) of Muslim Toledo in 1085, delivering to the Andalusian Muslims a debilitating defeat which came to portend more calamities to follow.

Ibn Hamdis, a self-imposed émigré from his fractious homeland, would now have to encounter face to face this Christian aggression which he had escaped back home. Whether monitoring events from the safety zone of the palace complex, or witnessing these battles in the company of the king and the military command, as some of his verses suggest, Ibn Hamdis from this point on fashioned his poetry in two very distinctive ways. First, by way of the lived experience of a *jahili*-like poet-warrior, he crafted his verses by drawing on his mastery of the classical poetic canons and by employing a creative intertextuality with the giants of Arabic panegyrics in order to inject contemporary meanings to his poems through evocations of real people and real events. Being in the company of, and in competition with, numerous talented and accomplished court poets compelled him to find his own particular voice, and this was done most effectively, once again, in the persona of the perennial Sicilian exile in search of the kindness and protection of a noble-minded patron. Second, the public poetry of Ibn Hamdis, that is, the panegyrics he composed at al-Mu'tamid's court, and those he would later compose to the Zirid princes of Ifriqiya, as will be discussed in the following chapters, embraced the cause of Islam in the face of what he viewed as Christian aggression. Ibn Hamdis assumed the role of the holy warrior poet, meshing pan-Islamic tropes and appeals with his powerful 'pan-Arab' proclivities, to borrow once again from modern parlance. As we will see, Ibn Hamdis will spend the last forty years of his eighty-year life criss-crossing the wider Maghreb in search of patrons in need of a court-poet. Most of his panegyrics would be composed to the last four Zirid princes who ruled from Mahdia, especially in their efforts to liberate Sicily from the Normans.

POETIC SPARRING: POET AS CLIENT, POET AS COMPETITOR

The thirteen years in Seville, as mentioned above, were for Ibn Hamdis not only professionally and artistically rewarding but also crucial in expanding his political consciousness that would bring a powerful element of 'worldliness' and relevance to an otherwise conservative adherence to the strictures of classical Arabic poetry. Above all, these years bestowed on the Sicilian exile a patron who was as much his protector as he was his soulmate. Both men shared similar life experiences, and both were shaped by a fervent and uncompromising fidelity and pride in Arabness, of noble birth and noble qualities (*hasab wa nasab*). Above all they shared a passion for poetry. Both patron and poet sparred, competed, and celebrated in what I have phrased previously as the digestion of millions of words, images, stock phrases, meters, half and full verses, whole poems, and diwans. Both men maintained until their last breath of life a blind devotion to the centuries-old canons of Arabic philology and poetics that provided them with language to celebrate victory and bemoan defeat. One could say that for Ibn Hamdis, al-Mu'tamid ibn 'Abbad represented the highest model of the *mamduh*, the subject of poetic praise. None of the dozens of his post-Seville panegyrics, composed to the very powerful Zirid princes or to military commanders and men of lesser rank, would display, as we shall see, such poetic mastery, credibility, and sincerity as did his poems composed at the Court of Seville.

This chapter ends with a translation of what may very well be Ibn Hamdis's finest panegyric. There is no indication of the time or occasion on which it was composed. What distinguishes it is that it is a poem written *by* a poet and *for* a poet. As much as it taps into the repository of familiar themes and tropes of the Arabic panegyric, it succeeds nonetheless in reaching poetic virtuosity and lyricism that encapsulate the bonds and affinities that defined the relationship between the Andalusian host and his Sicilian guest.

Ibn Hamdis moves nimbly from the amatory preface by way of the love song (*ghazal*), and on to the wine song and the battle scenes throughout all of which he entwines his verses of praise. He digs deep into his linguistic pouch to compose a poem replete with creative but complex uses of antitheses, puns, alliterations, allusions, analogies or similes, metaphors and metonomies, epithets and parallelisms.

The last two lines bring the praise to a laudatory crescendo; that his patron, al-Muʿtamid is a poet, the king of poets, blessed by God with the gift of language. In recalling that first night when Ibn Hamdis was put to the poetic test and passed, he now pays tribute to the poetic superiority of his master, the highest praise of all:

1 We would not have brought to our night any enticement from vestal virgins
   were it not for union with those possessing coquettishness or bashfulness;
2 Exposing their faces, they are radiant like the sun;
   but when covered, they remove the veil to resemble twinkling stars;
3 Many a black-eyed beauty whose glances are never betrayed,
   since their eyes render them victorious in the assault;
4 or a ruby-lipped beauty from whose saliva
   I [moistened and] quenched my scorching thirst.
5 Envied for her loveliness, you cannot relieve yourself from your passion for her,
   with a morning of hair shimmering in lacquered black;
6 Do not feel spared of annihilation caused by her dagger eyes,
   for it is a symptom of the essence of possessing the black/white eyes [of a gazelle];
7 Indeed I am a man who does not consider putting aside restraint
   from one whom platonic love does not arise;
8 I have never been seduced by sagging buttocks,
   nor have I lost my head over a waist that is not slender;
9 and would that a draught of nectar from a cluster of grapes [wine] be lacking,
   you would not find a life that is clear of distress;
10 If its sparkle were to be passed around in darkness,
   it would extinguish the dark of night with its hoariness and blaze;
11 Its strength increases twofold (*diʿf*)
   when the nights bring it to the threshold of becoming a mellow (*daʿf*) vintage;

12 The nose only hears from the whispers of its fragrance
the supplications [made] between sweetness and radiance.
13 When the boon companion takes a sip of it,
you imagine it like a falling star that has sunk into a moon;
14 Flames hover over the wine [as it sits] in the goblets
throwing sparks in fear of touching water;
15 Its brides (the spheres of the stars) mount the thrones of our hands
revealed between the flute and the lute;
16 When the curtain of night tears open at daybreak
and the foam that has formed on the surface of the river [of wine] dissipates,
17 the morning raises its open hand toward it,
catching the brightest stars like pearls on the horizons;
18 A life whose blessings I doffed in my ageing;
if only the nights had not doffed them from my life;
19 And it passed, and I did not recognize its reality,
as though it were the [mere] shadow of a listless bird;
20 By God, O mimosa tree, in my sleepless nights
have the gazelles napped in the shade of your branches?
21 Does one living in exile return to a nest [in your boughs],
one whose wings are trapped in the snares of fate?
22 My heart is within you, and were it in my capacity,
the glance of the eye would fly my body to you out of passion;
23 Say to the abode I long for
from where the nights removed my traces to the abode of distance,
24 [that] I received the munificence of Ibn ʻAbbad and he bound me
with hefty purses (*bidar*) from the full moons (*buduur*) which I possess in you.
25 The camel herders fastened our saddlebags to him,
and my commitment to his abode is beyond wavering.
26 My beginning with him was despairing
but word from him lifted my situation to hope;
27 Cutting short (*qasr*) the lives of the enemy is his to claim,
as well as striking the sword from the scalp to the base of their necks (*qisar*);

28 He only desires justice in affairs of governance
in accordance with what the All-Merciful has revealed in His suras.
29 He renders with his right hand favors
that vest good deeds with the finest San'ani garments;
30 If the earth one day were to appear with an outstretched palm,
it would never lack for rain after [he unleashes] his bounty;
31 He seeks refuge in firmly established power,
rubbing the nose of Time in the mud of its dishonesty;
32 The flow [of his munificence] does not slip away from the hands of his resolutions,
and he turns the heads of his enemies into sheathes for his sharpened swords;
33 Following in the line of his noble forebears,
[who are] lions mounted on stallions, moons hovering over shooting stars;
34 Destinies do not deem easy being uprooted from their lineage,
just as the hard-wooded nab' tree has no relation to the marshy low ground.
35 Death scowls in fear of encountering [these forbears],
while the frontier (*thugr*) laughs because of them, flashing shiny teeth (*thugar*);
36 O you who moisten the lance when the lances are thirsty,
with the shedding of blood from the fiercest lions,
37 were it not for your passion for battle,
then determination would not mount the back of danger with you;
38 Whenever lances ignite in flames they penetrate [the enemy's] armor
while deceptively reaching their souls;
39 and in your steadfastness in battle, with death terrified,
it only proves your resolve to face them;
40 How many a battleground in which the shining blades of swords rip apart
what no physician could stitch back together with needles;
41 from a massive legion for whom clear conquest has guaranteed
the humiliation of the enemy by ultimate victory and triumph;

42 You wave your banners on which there is a sweetness for war
that flap like the outstretched thirsty hands of bereaved mothers;
43 The tips of the spears reach their targets with rancor,
where the smoke of the dust [of battle] emits its sparks;
44 How many a heart does it have whose caldrons boil over
when the embers of striking fall on the neck;
45 It is as though from their blood all tracks of land
when their swords grow flaccid fall lifeless;
46 Plunging into the waves of death with sword unsheathed he casts lots
with the lions [of war] between [the light of] day and [darkness of] night;
47 In smiting the back of the neck you have created a mouth
in which you let speak the tongue of the sharp sword;
48 O, you, who reach the heights, every low ground [rises] with your noble rank,
you give sustenance to everyone in need with your openhandedness;
49 Has the abundance of your wealth and generosity been following
the tracks of your courage in [pursuing] the ferocious lions of war?
50 People who harbor hopes exclaim your magnanimity,
and they come in droves on their journeys in late day and early morning;
51 Just like the meadow, whenever its air is fresh,
that invites its strollers to whiff the fragrance of flowers at daybreak;
52 The sea gifts you of what it holds within,
and the sea, without a doubt, has a mine of pearls;
53 We stand humbled before the master of verse
to recite our poems embellished with impoverishment;
54 [a master] whom God has endowed with the beauty of speech;
for had Ibn Hujr* known him, he would have turned to stone (hajar).

[* Imru' al-Qays Ibn Hujr al-Kindi lived in the sixth century and was the most famous *jahili* poet.]

5

FROM THE DARK CLOUDS OF AL-ZALLAQA TO A SECOND EXILE

The capitulation in 1085 of the Muslims of Toledo, the ancient capital of the Visigothic Kingdom (418–720) that ruled the Iberian Peninsula and southern France before the Muslim Conquest, marked a major turning point in the history of al-Andalus, and to a lesser extent the wider Mediterranean world. It was not the result of a bloody, hard-fought battle, but of the consequences of political and historical tides starting to shift in favor of the Christian kings. Beyond the devastating psychological impact it had on the Muslim kingdoms and principalities struggling to survive, it strengthened the hand of Alfonso VI, King of Leon and Castile, in his dealings with his Christian rivals as well as his Muslim allies and enemies.

Modern historians of medieval Muslim Spain have well noted that the period of the petty kings, i.e., the ta'ifa era of the eleventh century, was distinguished for its cultural florescence in the burgeoning of scholarship and the arts, for economic prosperity arising from the production of crafts, agriculture, and trade, and for political disintegration. Not only were the petty kings fighting among themselves, but some even found themselves compelled to enter into alliances with the Christians for military back-up and economic support. Compounding these trespasses of religious and sectarian boundaries were significant numbers of conversions that added to the turbulence arising from ethnic rivalries, religious factionalism, and intra-royal family disputes. By the last decades of the century, the political disintegration of what remained of al-Andalus drew the attention, as Brian Catlos has described, of two powerful forces: the Christian warriors and the Berber armies of North Africa.

CONFRONTATION AT BADAJOZ: ENTER THE ALMORAVIDS

Alfonso VI, son of Fernando I (King of Leon and Count of Castile), reigned as King of Leon and Castile from 1072–1109. He ascended to power after conniving and feuding with his siblings over territory his father divided among all his children. His quest for territorial expansion throughout the Iberian Peninsula replicated closely earlier Muslim practices. He battled and fought off his Christian rivals, and then exploited the weaknesses and divisions among the Muslim petty kings. In something akin to turned tables, he instituted his father's system of a protection or treaty tax, *parias*, resembling the Islamic poll tax, *jizya*, which he imposed on conquered, subdued, or dependent Muslim kings and chieftains. In return for protection or military provisions, he exacted the heavy taxes that replenished his coffers and put pressure on the Muslim economies. His successes in Toledo, Valencia, and Aledo emboldened him to set his sights further in areas in the south.

Al-Mu'tamid ibn 'Abbad, meanwhile, found himself in a difficult situation, having expended much money and resources in rivaling his enemies to achieve his own territorial ambitions. As a result, he too entered into an alliance with Alfonso VI in the hopes of achieving his goal to rule over a reunited Al-Andalus. In early 1085, having failed to meet the deadline on payment of the *parias* as per the terms of the alliance, al-Mu'tamid earned the wrath of Alfonso, who was obviously strapped for cash, and a war of words erupted, leading to military confrontation. In an act of desperation, al-Mu'tamid followed Muslim rivals and allies by pleading for the assistance of the Berber warlords from across the Straits.

One of the first of these confrontations took place sometime after the occupation of Toledo in 1085 and before the major battle of al-Zallaqa in 1086. This skirmish took place at the fortress of Labit in the garrison town of Aledo located on the outskirts of the city of Almeria. Despite the fact that Alfonso's forces succeeded in capturing the fortress and won the battle, Ibn Hamdis composed a forty-line praise qasida to al-Mu'tamid celebrating his and his militia's safe return to Seville. Several lines in the poem evoking God's will in the battle's outcome, and drawing allusions to difficult battles in Islamic history, not to mention the prayer of thanks to God for al-Mu'tamid's safe return, more than suggest that this was not a major victory for the Muslims. Ibn Hamdis nonetheless employed the poetic device of turning what is ugly into beauty (*tajmil al-qabih*) by recounting the bravery of the soldiers and highlighting the righteousness and glory of their commander. What stands out prominently in this poem is the five-line ending in which the poet imbues the battle with the sanctity of jihad, the degree of which was not his custom before this time.

36 You launched a jihad for God in the most righteous manner;
other rulers have followed your example, but have fallen short.
37 While they spend their nights in the company of wine and the music of the lute,
sturdy war-horses and chains of mail are your nocturnal companions.
38 The aromas of exotic perfumes exude in their midst,
while dust and blood bedaub your mantle.
39 A thirsty garden has bestowed upon you a garland of praises,
but how seldom does it pray for rain.
40 I rest assured that your power is all embracing;
your safe abode is the sweet life and your generosity the river of paradise.

(Diwan #120: 194–197)

This closing segment is an unusual departure in Ibn Hamdis's poetry. Ibn Hamdis was highly successful, like all the great poets of the neo-classical era of Arabic poetry, in moving from one mode to another smoothly and subtly in ways that the profane aspects (wine, women, music, sensual pleasures, etc.) would not appear to compromise the credibility of the poem or disturb the religious sensibilities or the political stances of his audience, especially since many would be familiar with the bawdy conventions of Arabic poetry. These closing lines of the *Labit* qasida depart from Ibn Hamdis's poetic practice in that he casts the binary of the profane with the religious (in the evocation of jihad) in stark opposition to each other, and here he uncustomarily privileges the religious over the profane, understandable given the context and occasion of the poem.

Another curious feature of this qasida is the brief, if somewhat cryptic, mention in the introduction to the poem of the Almoravids who had joined forces with al-Mu'tamid in this battle. Across the Mediterranean Sea the Almoravids (Arabic: *al-Murabitun*) rose to political dominance in the Maghreb in the middle of the eleventh century and remained a powerful force in both North Africa and Spain for nearly a century. Ethnically Berber, their leaders hailed from the Lamtuna tribe of the Sanhaja Berber confederation. Their power stemmed from their control of the Saharan trade routes, and it increased with a religious populism directed toward the Berber tribes. The movement was founded by 'Abdallah Ibn Yasin who established their military headquarters in the southern [today] Moroccan city of Marrakesh. Their appeal, having successfully taken root with numerous Berber tribes throughout the wider Maghreb, encompassed a populist fundamental brand of Sunni Maliki Islam that denounced decadence, injustice, and deviation from the right path. However, the early and unexpected death of the movement's founder, Ibn Yasin, in a battle against the Barghawata Berbers, paved the way for Yusuf Ibn Tashufin who, from his capital at Marrakesh, succeeded in bringing much of the Maghreb under his control. The Almoravids, as we will see more in detail, were highly instrumental in holding back the Christian reconquest in al-Andalus.

THE BATTLE OF AL-ZALLAQA

The Battle of al-Zallaqa (Sagrajas) of 1086 brought together multiple forces and would become a milestone in medieval Spanish history. A combination of militias of the Spanish reconquest, Castilian, Galician, etc., along with once-warring but now hurriedly united battalions of the Muslim ta'ifas, met on the battlefield in the company of the ominous and formidable Berber army from the Maghreb. From what was anticipated to be a duel between Alfonso VI and al-Mu'tamid, there emerged a triumvirate of military might that competed for power and control over vast stretches of land populated by a hodgepodge of different ethnicities, faiths, professions, shifting identities, and fickle political loyalties. The fifteenth-century Arab historian Muhammad al-Himyari has bequeathed a colorful and detailed picture of it in his geographical encyclopedia, *Kitab al-Rawd al-Mi'tar* (the Book of the Perfumed Garden, composed c. 1460).

Al-Himyari's account of the battle is written in linear progression and it inserts direct quotations and word-for-word messages that add an audible quality to his text that is replete with vivid visual images of people, places, and behind the scene activities, from plotting and scheming, spying, recruiting of fighters, and hosts of merchants seeking to make a profit from the hustle and bustle of war. Al-Himyari begins with a description of the locale of the battle and the reasons why tensions between the two parties came to a head: al-Mu'tamid fails to make [scheduled] payments in terms of his treaty with Alfonso; an enraged Alfonso, in an act of revenge, announces his intention to lodge his pregnant wife between the palace of al-Zahra' and the Mosque of Cordoba, sacred sites of the now-defeated but still much revered Cordoban caliphate; and al-Mu'tamid, in his fit of rage against this insult to Islam, kills and hangs in public an insolent Jewish emissary dispatched by Alfonso who had the misfortune of being the bearer of bad news.

As both Muslims and Christians mobilize for war, al-Mu'tamid makes his appeal to neighboring princes and chieftains of Bajados, Granada, and Cordoba to send their senior jurists to join a delegation, headed by his own chief minister, Abu Bakr Ibn Zaydun, to cross the Straits and plead with the Almoravids to join his jihad. Yusuf complies and leads his massive army to cross into al-Andalus. They are festively received by local communities, with merchants seeing in them opportunities to sell their wares, and unemployed young men lining up at the marketplace to volunteer to join the holy war in order to reap its heavenly and earthly rewards. As he marches with his army toward

Seville in grand procession, as al-Himyari describes it, he is greeted by al-Mu'tamid who embraces him at the gates of the palace in a public display of unity and solidarity. They swear an oath to defeat the infidels, and then they retreat to their stations.

Among the most dramatic scenes in al-Himyari's account are those that depict Christian bishops and monks marching in procession while hoisting crosses and bibles as the Christian soldiers prepare for war. It is these groups, al-Himyari informs us, who prodded Alfonso to trespass the sacred spaces of the Muslims. No longer a regional skirmish for extending one's territory and control, al-Zallaqa would come to bear all the signs of crusade and jihad. Only several decades prior to this battle, Alfonso's father, Count Fernando of Castile, had dispatched a message to his religious nemeses:

> We … demand our land, which a long time ago you conquered and which you have inhabited for as long as had been ordained [by God]. Now He has given us victory over you on account of your wickedness. Depart to your own shores [of North Africa] and give our land up to us. For there is no good in your living with us any longer, nor will we turn away from you until God has judged between you and us.
>
> (Quoted in Brian Catlos, *Kingdoms of Faith*: 221)

And it would be a mere ten years later when Pope Urban II initiated the First Crusade with promises of forgiveness of sins and eternal rewards to all those who fought to reclaim the holy lands in Jerusalem, as well to those who joined in the struggle to dispel the 'Moors' from Spain. On the Muslim side, it should be borne in mind, both the plea to Yusuf to cross into al-Andalus and his positive response to it were made in both the spirit and language of jihad and the defense of the faith against the Christian infidels. Al-Himyari reports that in observing Islamic scriptural codes of warfare, Yusuf dispatched an emissary to Alfonso inviting him to convert to Islam or pay the poll tax. His narrative goes on to describe how an indignant Alfonso began his attack deceptively on Friday, not only in violation of an agreement to Saturday both parties had made, but more significantly as an insulting display of disrespect toward the Muslim sabbath. After an abundance of battlefield detail, al-Himyari's narrative concludes with a Muslim victory but one that leaves a seriously wounded al-Mu'tamid as well as a wounded Alfonso who, in the dark of night, makes a cowardly escape with a number of his officers.

As was the custom of the royal court, a celebration of the victory was held with full public pageantry on the Friday following the battle, and the court poets were called upon to compose and deliver their poems of praise as part of the festivities. Ibn Hamdis rose to the occasion with a vintage traditional tripartite qasida. The poem commences with an introductory wine song replete with stock images of the quality of the grape, the richness and scents of the wine, the company of young maidens and boon companions, melodious music, and nightly imbibing. This segment ends with a smooth transition from nocturnal inebriation to morning sobriety when the poet-lover is transformed into poet-warrior. Prepared for battle, clad in armor, brandishing sword in hand, he mounts his black stallion and embarks on his journey through hostile terrain. The poet then nimbly shifts to the praise that begins with his own refuge, "in the abode of Ibn 'Abbad" (line 17), a poetic verse that draws attention to the poet's departure from Sicily. The litany of al-Mu'tamid's many qualities is interrupted by a brief invective against Alfonso (lines 27–28) and a one-line acknowledgement of Yusuf Ibn Tashufin's contribution to the victory (line 29). To bring an immediacy and excitement to his poem, Ibn Hamdis weaves in verses recounting actual details of the battle, i.e., Alfonso's scheming and escape, enhancing the overall impact and credibility of the panegyric:

1 I clothed the dear little daughters of the vine
with embellishments the remains of abodes once donned;
2 I followed the path of al-Hakami* in pursuing them;
How could I turn away from this wise man's theme?
[* Abu Nuwas (al-Hasan ibn Hani al-Hakim (d. 815)), early 'Abbasid poet famed for his wine songs.]
3 How can abandoned ruins surpass the quality of fresh wine
that exudes musk into the breath of fresh air?
4 The love of wine is renewed in every heart,
since wine polishes away the rust of anxieties.
5 In the days of old, I longed for the pleasures
[that awaited me] in the ancient castle.
6 If I thirsted, then my cup was returned to me,
just as the full breast is returned to the weaning child.

7 I would not ask a muted ruin to converse,
as though it possessed the power to speak.
8 I would instead seek out melodies from a lute
that arouse pleasures in the bosom of a gazelle.
9 A fine vintage would put to sleep my drinking companions from drunkenness,
but with it I could chase away their slumber.
10 The drinking companions would awake, as the eye of early morning
has the twinkling residue of the dark night;
11 as though the early morning, facing its darkness,
is a combatant who stares down his opponent in disdain;
12 as though the East, between the one and the other,
is a battle line, across which Zanj and Rum come face to face.
13 The night [was] like a black stallion, but when the light of day broke loose
it turned into a young [weaned] camel on the attack.
14 Throughout night's darkness we crossed a vast terrain,
on a camel with flesh stripped from the bone.
15 With its hooves dripping in blood, we crossed the open desert with her,
leaving our traces [firmly implanted] on the sand.
16 We wandered from town to town,
like people whose souls have been comforted by the body's fatigue.
17 Then in the abode of Ibn 'Abbad, we alighted,
and we were regaled with munificence from one so resolute.
18 Such that kings would lower their eyes
to pay homage to the aura of the mightiest king.
19 Noble qualities are neatly arranged within his ranks,
and you would think that they were the [brightest] stars.
20 Acts of generosity flow from his fingertips,
and you would think that they were the [fullest] rain clouds.
21 If hopes come to him thirsting with passion,
then they leave quenched by the [generous] dew of his hand.
22 Where generous men are relegated to oblivion,
he brings forth a memory that travels in the mouth of time to come.

23 The sharpness of his vision whispers privately to him
secrets that are hidden deep within the heart.
24 O scion of [the royal tribe of] Lakhm,
whose members are moons that shine brightest among the noblest tribes.
25 When they are generous, they bring downpours of generosity,
and when they are gentle, they erect mountains of gentility.
26 In your right hand is a sword which is inviolable,
and by using it you safeguard that which is sacred,
27 in a battle in which Alfonso encountered the opponent,
one who causes havoc on the soul of [his] adversary.
28 He took cover in the dark of night, and then fled in fear,
with a terror that could shatter the ears of an ostrich.
29 Because of Yusuf, endowed with bravery (*ba's*), Alfonso was made to taste misery (*bu's*),
and the sweetness of a graced life was rendered bitter.
30 The serpentine blades tore him apart with their sharp teeth,
so, ask the sound (*salim*) night about the one bitten (*salim*) by the snake.
31 Your monotheism dissuaded him of his [trinitarian] polytheism,
snipping at the hands of [his] fear, snarling with anger.
32 Insulted, he watched you as you grin like a hunting hound
who even when it yawns it bares its fangs.
33 In early morning he came with crosses that lead infidels astray,
having concocted the schemes of a mongrel army.
34 It was as though they [appeared] like devils,
but [it was] you who hurled at them the fire of stars.
35 Infidels, their battle coats are concealed with armor,
but the whiff of their odor gives them away.
36 A tyrant [even] to them who leads them to their demise,
and woe unto the tyrant!
37 He brought them to graze on a pasture of washij* trees, and they tottered about,
and such are the consequences of evil grazing.
[* A kind of tree from the wood of which swords were made.]
38 He led them to watering holes amidst the sharp lances,
and like a water boy he served the waters of death from the well.

39 And then when he came to you with a people from Aad*
along you came with the howling destructive wind.
[* 'Aad and Thamud, evoked by Arab poets as ancient Arabian tribes in the Jahiliyya, here serve as metaphors for 'pagans.' Quran references to God punishing the people of Aad: Surat al-Haqqa 69: 6; and Surat Aad 89: 6–9.]
40 You rekindled the fires of battle,
and its moans cried out that they were the sparks of hell.
41 With the gallop of sturdy horses there arose a dark gloom,
by which they clothed the maimed (*sarim*) with the night (*sarim*).
42 The robe of the air was frayed at the edges,
and the face of the earth was scorched at the surface.
43 The ascending Khatt spears were inebriated,
until every pliant straight arrow was arched.
44 They drank only from the wine of collarbones,
and they inhaled only the scent of head wounds.
45 So, pray to your God who is worshipped, and make a sacrifice
to Him of their leaders, one after the other.
46 And celebrate with divine guidance, and prepare for the enemy
the punishment of war, with the most painful of pain.
(Diwan #283: 435–438)

Aside from the honor of participating in the celebrations of the Zallaqa victory, Ibn Hamdis undoubtedly faced a daunting challenge. If al-Himyari's gruesome details in his narrative are correct, and if they were known among the members of al-Mu'tamid's Court during and following the battle, the poet was tasked to accentuate the positive and camouflage the negative, if only to reassure a nervous audience living in perilous times. Al-Himyari describes a fierce and bloody battle in which heavy casualties were suffered on both sides. Not only was Alfonso severely wounded in the knee, resulting in a limp he would carry for the rest of his life, al-Mu'tamid himself suffered serious gashes to his head and his right hand, as well as a stab wound to his side. Assuming that the victorious king was present at the celebration, the poet would need to draw on all of his poetic skills to deliver a panegyric that needed to be credibly received by an otherwise skeptical audience. In addition, Al-Himyari's narrative is punctuated with references to lingering suspicions between Al-Mu'tamid's commanding officers and the Almoravids. It should be noted that prior to this most significant eruption of hostilities between the Castilians and the 'Abbadids, several of the Andalusi warlords, as well as members of al-Mu'tamid's own inner circle of advisors, cautioned him against entering into an alliance with the primitive and Quran-brandishing fundamentalist "Saharans." It was in the midst of attempts to dissuade him of this alliance that al-Mu'tamid purportedly uttered his famous and oft-quoted reply: "Better to herd camels in the desert than to graze pigs among the Christians."

At the root of 'Abbadid suspicions about their Almoravid co-religionists, aside from their populist fundamentalist religious tendencies, was the belief that the North African Berbers were unfamiliar with the Iberian terrain, an assumption shared by the Castilians. The belief was that they would be unable to lead the way into battle and, therefore, should follow al-Mu'tamid's command. These suspicions came into public view following the battle when a disagreement arose between al-Mu'tamid and Yusuf over whether or not to pursue and kill the wounded and fleeing Alfonso. Although Yusuf lost the argument and directed his troops back to the Maghreb, he would eventually return to exact his vengeance.

One could easily imagine at this time that Ibn Hamdis, haunted by the memories of a chaotic Sicily caught between the political divisions among his compatriots and the ominous threats of an invading army, was now living these realities head on. Gone was the 24-year-old aspiring poet living a privileged life in his homeland, where he was at a safe distance from the events of conflict unraveling far from Syracuse and Noto, where he was romantically immersed in his secluded world of Arabic poetry that celebrated Arab warriors, lovers, and poets of pure blood and noble qualities. Ibn Hamdis of the 'Abbadid Court in 1086, was now immersed in the thick of battle where his once preferred idyllic verses of Arabic poetics demanded a new immediacy and a change in course.

The concluding two lines of the Zallaqa qasida underscore the theme of a religious war, an Islamic jihad, and from this time forward Ibn Hamdis's panegyrics would assume a very local and targeted political tone. The specter of the Christian monks as well as Yusuf's soldiers brandishing their scriptural symbols into battle convinced the exiled Sicilian poet that his beloved homeland, recalled and evoked in classical poetic terms of endearment, would not be wrested merely from the grip of a Christian conquest by extolling the virtues of the Arabian heroes of poetic lore. He had become undoubtedly convinced that the might of Almoravid religious zeal, although much at odds with the secular humanist thrust of Arabic poetry, would be more effective in bringing him home.

THE FALL OF THE 'ABBADIDS OF SEVILLE

Five years later, in 1091, Yusuf Ibn Tashufin crossed the Straits with his formidable army and returned to al-Andalus with a vengeance, aimed at both a sinful 'Abbadid court culture and Christian infidelity. Many of the remaining Muslim ta'ifas submitted with or without a fight, while al-Mu'tamid held his ground as long as he could. But history was working against him, and in the end he was forced to submit to his fate. His kingdom was overrun, his court abolished, and several of his sons were killed in battle. The last 'Abbadid king of Seville was sent into exile across the sea, along with the surviving members of his family, to a prison complex in the small town of Aghmat, a military outpost on the southern outskirts bordering Marrakesh, the headquarters and new capital city of the Almoravids.

It was only natural that 'Abd al-Jabbar Ibn Hamdis flee the smoldering ruins of Seville and follow the tracks of the defeated royal family and its entourage. His flight from the gilded life of a court poet constituted a second exile. He crossed the Strait not only to seek safe terrain but, more compellingly, to resume his career as a professional poet. From a series of verses that made their way into his diwan, we know that the forever loyal Ibn Hamdis maintained contact with is former patron through an exchange of correspondence as well as attempted visits to Aghmat. The diwan contains two pairs of exchanges, each consisting of a letter penned by al-Mu'tamid and a reply by his loyal and beloved court poet. Naturally, the letters and the replies were composed in the form of the classical qasida, in which Ibn Hamdis, reminiscent of that first encounter on that dark late-summer night thirteen years ago, responded to al-Mu'tamid's verses employing the same meter and rhyme. The one pair begins with a poem that, drawing from the language and emotion of the love-song, and bemoaning the treacherous times the imprisoned king had fallen on, is nonetheless a humble and heartful letter of apology after having learned that Ibn Hamdis had come to visit him but was refused entry by a servant who misled him into thinking that al-Mu'tamid was not there. Ibn Hamdis's reply, as would be expected, expresses his sympathy and reaffirms his loyalty.

The other pair, and we do not know which of the two actually came first, is a powerful ode in which the deposed and exiled king expresses a nostalgia for a glorious past:

> 10 Would that I knew whether I shall ever again spend a night
> with a garden before me and a pool of water behind me,
> 11 in a grove of olive trees, the heritage of nobility
> where doves coo and birds warble?
> (Diwan #152: 268; Monroe: 200)

Ibn Hamdis, having himself suffered the loss of a homeland and forced into exile, waxes philosophical in his attempt to console his patron:

> 3 Our affairs run counter to the decrees [of Fate.]
> while Fate is at times just to man and at times unjust.

In verses further down, he conjures apocalyptic images of a world turned upside down through which he attempts to poeticize the shared fate of loss and exile both men were suffering:

> 10 Until the present no full-grown camels on whom a rider gallops at dawn
> have ever alarmed the night-flying sandgrouse,
> 11 nor has a generous man ever rejoiced at the wealth
> that a poor man puts into his hands.
> (Diwan #152: 269; Monroe: 202)

I draw to a close Ibn Hamdis's Seville chapter by citing a poem he composed to al-Mu'tamid during the first year of his imprisonment. Like the verses of the epistolary poems cited above, there is no evocation of jihad, or any anguished mention of the current political realities, such as the increasing threat of the Christian conquest or the rise of a fundamental religious conservatism that would take a dim view of profane court life and poetry. In these post-Zallaqa verses, king and subject, praised-patron and praiser-poet, speak to each other on equal footing, poet to poet, in the exclusive language of the classical Arabic qasida and all the emotions it was capable of eliciting for such occasions. The qasida, thirty-six lines long, reads less as a panegyric and more like an elegy, in spite of the fact that the patron/king was still alive.

First, there is the overwhelming melancholic mood that permeates the entire poem. There is no attempt to make what is ugly beautiful. Second, there are verses of nostalgia and the *ubi sunt* motif that recall the days of noble Arab (read: 'Abbadid) glory, as well as apocalyptic images to express the sudden twists of fate (line 18: "Are the walking of mountains and the scattering of stars signs that the Day of Reckoning has drawn near?") that are more common to elegy than panegyric. Third, we see repeatedly the elegiac motif of (*tafajju'*), the poet's personal anguish over the suffering experienced by the subject of the praise. Finally, the last three lines of the poem begin with the poet's admission of his 'passing on from the conventional praise' and ends with his explicit but curious choice of *marathi* (elegy: sing. *marthiya*), a term applied more often than not to 'elegy,' to describe this poem which is, in essence, an expression of fealty to the still-living patron-king with a promise never to forget him in his poetry. It is well within the realm of possibility that Ibn Hamdis chose this particular term to indicate the sub-genre of the poem instead of the customary '*madh*' merely to fit the meter, or even as a synecdoche to mean poetry in general. But this was a poet who mastered the nuances of an ocean of words and phrases, a poet well known and highly respected among philologists and anthologists, and his choice of '*marthiya*' to express his feelings is richly significant:

1 May Death put an end to my life as long as I be unmindful [of you]
while you linger imprisoned in chains.
2 If I cannot match the rain clouds in shedding tears for you,
then my own gravesite will not be watered by even the lightest drizzle.

3 My heart has been stripped bare when once it was donned with laughter,
and now I am draped only in crying eyes.
4 The joy that once filled my days of happiness no longer obeys me,
and my sorrow at this time of infamy does not rebel.
5 How can I find consolation over you,
hearing reports that would make the most mighty of men cry tears of blood?
6 Your chains have been forged in iron
where there was once a helpful hand against those who transgressed.
7 A blessing [from God] was bestowed upon you without you asking for it,
and with it you pierced the dark night and brought us morning light.
8 You prepared for this catastrophe [lit: exposed your leg] and in so doing
you severed the necks and clipped the forelocks [of the enemy or horses].
9 They stopped in their tracks bogged down by weight (*thiqal*) and you were given no room to advance,
as if you could not prod lightly loaded (*khifaf*) horses into action.
10 The stomping of black steeds kept you awake at night,
and when you slept the swords kept you company with their chants.
11 I would never be alarmed if it were to be exclaimed: O Muhammad,
the arrow of fate is pointed directly toward you.
12 Now the mighty Sword of Battle spends the night in prison tucked in his sheathe,
and the morning is stripped of the ornaments of authority.
13 A Lion of War has been enslaved there unjustly,
one who was once the aggressor in the face of the lion.
14 O Mountain, in your day you crushed the hardest boulders;
were you not solidly grounded in [the bedrock of] power?
15 You were cut short before your mandate was completed,
one in which Fate tiptoed barefoot out of respect for you.

———

25 How many tyrants are there whose souls you snatched
and those whom you kept alive with points of your lances
lodged in their chests.
26 On the battlefield they smite and they spike,
while their stallions trample on the bodies of the fallen
enemy.
27 They pass the days of joy and then come the opposite,
and oh! what a difference there is.
28 When you rose to power you took command with righteous
guidance,
just as your right hand directed the course of battle.
29 Even when you secluded yourself in your tent,
it was only words of adulation that crossed men's lips.
30 I pass through the doors of [your] palaces,
and I find myself in secret confiding with one who is far
away.
31 I recite verses that I usually do not recite,
"Revive with rain the remains of abandoned abodes."
32 I call out to their dwellers, one lord after another,
and after them I [have] become an elderly client.
33 Stories of ruins, whenever I return to them,
I unleash on them my tears and my verses.
34 I'm now passed in praising like the vanishing cloud,
after having embellished deserted encampments with an
embroidery of spring flowers.
35 I will bleed my eyes with sleeplessness as a punishment
should I ever cease to shed tears for you,
36 and I will deny myself a salubrious life
because you live on and are worthy of my praises (elegies).

(Diwan #335: 530–533)

6

1091: *ANNUS HORRIBILIS* AND THE SECOND DESERT CROSSING

If the fall of Seville to the Almoravids and the degrading imprisonment of his royal patron and poetic boon companion were not enough to register 1091 as a most horrendous year in the life of ʻAbd al-Jabbar Ibn Hamdis, then the conquest of the fortress town of Castrogiovanni as well as the soon to follow hometown of Syracuse and the neighboring towns of Noto by the Norman militias would certainly make it so. And, closer to home, Ibn Hamdis suffered in the chaos that disrupted his professional life the loss of his beloved Jawhara, slave girl, concubine, and faithful companion who, it has been conjectured, was gifted to the poet from al-Muʻtamid.

Ibn Hamdis penned three elegies to Jawhara, (one surviving only in fragment) that vary in length, meter, lyric, and temperament. The first, cited below in full translation, was the shorter of the two completed poems and most likely having been composed soon after the poet received news of her drowning. It is assumed that Jawhara followed him on a later ship when he fled Seville. Its brevity and short meter suggest that it was a spontaneous and highly emotional response to her demise:

1 The builder of life destroys its abodes;
  is there anything in this world that rests eternal?
2 If nations have come and gone before us,
  then they are no more than spirits borrowed and returned.

3 You view life as though it were a forest,
where lions, like our fates, roam in our midst.
4 If our days make peace, then life's days do not,
while fate's nights wage war on us.
5 Both have afflicted upon us the agony of longing for a sweet companion,
the very mention of her kills me, but keeps her alive.
6 I utter her name and tears race down my cheeks,
as though I could only keep pace with my grief.
7 O sea, so callously have you made cheap
the one so dear to me, and not merely through purchase.
8 Jawhara [was my jewel], and my heart was a shell for her
that kept her close [to me] and well protected.
9 You beckoned her to drown deep within you
while I spent the night on shore sobbing over her loss.
10 As the scent of a sweet fragrance perfumed her hair
and the tint of kohl laced her eyes,
11 the waves embraced her and then took her away
from the warm caress from which her soul has departed.
12 May God protect me from the water and earth,
and from the laws of the two elements that sentenced her to die.
13 The one made her perish and the other transformed her;
so how can I ransom her from these forces of nature?

(Diwan #325: 517–518)

Bereft of his beloved companion, separated from his family, and stripped of his prestigious position as court poet, Ibn Hamdis found himself once again on the road. His brief sojourn in Aghmat in the south of Morocco to visit and console a defeated and humiliated al-Muʿtamid was soon followed by the long and arduous trek back east. The distance of a thousand miles that lie between Marrakesh, just north of Aghmat, and the port city of Bejaia (Bijaya, Bougie) on the northeastern coast of Algeria covered rugged mountain ranges and vast stretches of desert that undoubtedly qualified in the eyes of the lifelong aficionado of Arabic poetry as that hostile terrain so passionately evoked, described, and decried in the hundreds of thousands of verses of the classical and neoclassical Arabic qasida.

INTERMISSION AT QAL'AT BANI HAMMAD

Ibn Hamdis's first stop of major professional significance was at the fortress town of Qal'at Bani Hammad, situated in the Hodna mountain range south of Bejaia at an elevation close to five thousand feet. The town was founded in 1014 by Hammad ibn Buluggin, a member of the Sanhaja Berber clan of the Banu Ziri. It should be recalled that before departing for Egypt in 972, the Fatimid caliph of Ifriqiya, al-Mu'izz li Din Allah, divided the vast lands of his realm and apportioned to Buluggin ibn Ziri the largest and most prosperous province of Ifriqiya, as well as any territory he could seize from the rival Zanata Berbers. Some twelve years later, in 984, Buluggin was killed on his way back from a successful campaign against the Zanata in the western Maghreb cities of Fez and Sijilmasa. A decade later, Buluggin's grandson and heir to the throne, Badis ibn al-Mansur ibn Buluggin (r. 995–1016), dispatched his uncle, Hammad ibn Buluggin, with a sizeable militia to continue military campaigns against the Zanata in the central Maghreb, with the incentive that he could rule any territories he captured from them. In 1008, Hammad gained control of areas stretching from the Hodna mountains and their adjacent plains all the way north to the small fishing port of Bejaia on the Mediterranean coast. Once settled in the area, Hammad declared for himself a kingdom independent of his cousins in Kairouan and named its capital Qal'at Bani Hammad.

By the time Ibn Hamdis arrived there after a long and sorrowful journey, he contacted its ruler, al-Mansur ibn al-Nasir ibn 'Alnas (r. 1088–1104). Al-Mansur inherited his mandate to rule from his father, al-Nasir ibn 'Alnas (r. 1062–1088) who is credited for having turned the fortress town into a palatine city with an extensive project of public and private buildings, and for transforming the fishing port of Bejaia into a second capital city. He chose this site not only because it was nearly inaccessible to invasion by rival Berber and Arab tribes, but its location served as a strategic outlet to the sea. Al-Mansur continued to build on his father's projects of erecting palaces and creating irrigation networks that provided water for his elaborate patchwork of gardens. After the first years of rule, al-Mansur came to preside over his realm mainly from Bejaia, but he maintained Qal'at Bani Hammad in full operation.

One can imagine Ibn Hamdis happening upon a mini metropolitan oasis after crossing the desert expanses of North Africa when he arrived at Qal'at Bani Hammad. With its well-fortified walls, mosques, palaces, and well-watered gardens, the Hammadid kingdom of al-Nasir and al-Mansur, encompassing a bustling mountain village and a thriving port, had become a major crossroads for traveling merchants, pilgrims, and mercenaries, as well as a sanctuary for political and religious dissidents and exiles. The Hammadids, early on, had proclaimed their loyalty to the 'Abbasid caliphate in Baghdad in their rejection of Fatimid Shi'ism, earning the wrath, no doubt, of the Fatimid caliphs and their supporters and deputies. To add fuel to the fire, their soon-thereafter gradual but unequivocal declaration of independence from the Zirid Court in Mahdia rendered them official enemies of the rulership in Ifriqiya. Scholars and theologians from the wider Maghreb flocked to the Hammadid kingdom where they found comfort and patronage in a secure Sunni stronghold. Also, the growing strength of the Christian conquests and the fall of petty kingdom after petty kingdom throughout the Iberian Peninsula propelled waves of emigration of Muslims, Jews, and Mozarabs many of whom passed through or settled in the Hammadid kingdom.

Adding to Ibn Hamdis's relief and possible delight at landing at Qal'at Bani Hammad was the presence of a Christian community, not of course the Christians of the Reconquest armies of Sicily and al-Andalus he would vilify in his later poetry, but common folk with whom Muslims shared a common life back in his native Syracuse and his adopted home in Seville. Late-eighteenth and early nineteenth-century French colonial historians and archaeologists have debated the presence and nature of this community, with one theory holding that it was one of the last indigenous Christian communities of North Africa before they were eliminated by the Almohads in the twelfth century; another argument holds that it merely was one made up of Christian mercenaries and slaves. Beyond the speculation there remains evidence of correspondence between al-Nasir ibn 'Alnas and Pope Gregory VII, as well as a thriving church and bishopric that enjoyed the protection of the Hammadid Palace.

We have no historical accounts on when Ibn Hamdis arrived and how long he stayed in the Hammadid Kingdom. It can be safely assumed that it was not his intention to settle there. Despite its relative safety, prosperity, and impressive level of arts and culture, its location in a remote area was too far from the exiled poet's intended destination: Sicily. His diwan includes three panegyrics to its ruler, al-Mansur. One is a proper panegyric, and two read more like description poems that pay homage less to the ruler than to the royal palace (or palaces).

The overall tenor and content of the poems support the assumption that Ibn Hamdis was merely passing through. The poems lack any suggestion of an intimacy or bonding with the subject of his praise, and there are no references or allusions to local or contemporaneous details, a hallmark of his poetry. Other than a few mentions of al-Mansur by name, there are no reports of actual people or events. References to time are limited to evocations of ancient Near Eastern, Persian, and Roman (or Byzantine) empires, as well as events in early Islamic history. There are, most significantly, no references of specifically Christian enemies, such as those of the Spanish and Norman Sicilian conquests, and this underscores the remoteness and insignificance of the Hammdid kingdom to Ibn Hamdis's trajectory. The first poem, the panegyric proper (Diwan #284: 439–441), consists of forty-two lines that can be divided into two segments: a wine song (lines 1–19) and the praise (lines 20–41). The praise focuses on two qualities: generosity and bravery in battle. Both are built on stock phrases that would read to a student of Arabic poetry as generic. Also, given that al-Mansur's battles would have been limited to fighting off minor incursions from nomadic tribesmen or even his fuming rival Zirid cousins further east, the verses extolling al-Mansur's gallantry and defense of the faith would be understood or appreciated solely for their artistic craft.

What is indeed remarkable about Ibn Hamdis's Hammadid poetry are the two qasidas that display his exceptional skills at the poetic subgenre of description, at which both Arabic Spanish and Sicilian poetry excelled. The *wasf*, it should be recalled, was a cluster of verses within the classical Arabic qasida that broke away and developed as an independent genre in its own right. It was often used in the *rahil* segment where the poet would display his poetic talents and rhetorical skills by describing a desert flower or an emaciated she-camel. As an independent art form, it appeared more often than not as a short fragment (*qit'a*) ranging from two to eight lines or more, or as a monothematic or occasional poem. The *wasf* was widely practiced among philologists and court scribes as demonstrations of their linguistic and literary skills. Although the poems are labeled as panegyrics to al-Mansur in Ibn Hamdis's diwan, they are actually poems that sing the praises of his architectural achievements.

Despite the fact that there are no indications of which building he is describing, the richness of these poems nonetheless lies in the vivid descriptions of their architectural features and the exquisite display of metaphors and similes the poet employs in bringing them alive. The archaeological work undertaken in the late- nineteenth and early twentieth-century yields important details on the palace's footprint and overall structure, with evidence of vertical niches, shell-shaped domes and honeycomb vaulting (*muqarnas*), with ramps and water channels (*shadirwan*), decorations of carved plaster, painted frescos, polychrome tiles, bronze, jewels of gold and silver, colored glassware and cut crystal and marble sculptures, all vividly described in these two poems. The dominance of the lion statues and motifs allows Ibn Hamdis to explode in metaphoric language, including the personification of lions, birds, and celestial bodies to give the poems a lively animation that pays tribute to Hammadid creativity and patronage. Islamic art historian D. Fairchild Ruggles has interrogated the conventional thesis of earlier art historians that the Hammadid palaces were built on the influences of North African Aghlabid, Fatimid, and Zirid models, and has argued that the Hammadids were as much influenced by Andalusi precedents, especially in the much revered and imitated Cordoban example of the palace of Madinat al-Zahra'. Given the traffic of exiled Andalusians heading points east, and the knowledge and exuberance that the recently exiled Ibn Hamdis displayed in "reading" the Hammadid palaces, Ruggles's thesis stands firm, and we can imagine both the delight and nostalgia for al-Andalus that inspired Ibn Hamdis to compose these verses:

1 Construct a grand reception hall in the palace of government
where one's presence there is graced by your majesty;
2 A palace, one that if you endow the eye of a blind man with its light,
he would return home with full sight.
3 [A palace] whose fragrance is derived from the essence of life,
and in no time does it bestow resurrection to the bones.
4 The mere mention of it makes one forget what was [once] elegant and radiant,
as it surpasses the ancient palace and castle of King Naaman*
[* Aramaean commander of the Syrian army.]
5 If its beauty was placed next to Khosrow's Iwan,*
then nothing [of the ancient palace] would be recalled.
[* Khrosow Anushirvan, King of Kings of sixth-century Sassanian Iran; the iwan is an arched reception room that once formed part of his Sasanian palace complex in Ctesiphon.]
6 Its pavilions are more imposing than those of all the ancient Persians
who were master architects and built majestic buildings.
7 Then, time passed on to the Romans,
but they could not build for their kings the likes [of what al-Mansur has built].
8 You remind us of Paradise
when you show us the chambers and pavilions you have erected.
9 [Because of this Paradise] those who do good increase their good deeds,
and thus look forward to a celestial garden and robes of silk.
10 And those who do evil have been guided to the straight path,
and their good deeds forgive their sins.
11 It is a star in the galaxy of stars;
it is perched above the moon and it has elevated al-Mansur.
12 I observe it closely and I behold the most wondrous of sights,
and in turning away from it I am left blinded by its light.
13 I feel as though I am dreaming in Paradise
where I catch sight of how grand is its king.

14 And when the handmaidens open its doors for me,
they welcome their guests with [melodious] chirping.
15 Lions clutch with their teeth the door rings
by which they lure their mouths to gnash.
16 They appear as though they are standing guard
to prevent those without permission to enter.
17 Fanciful thoughts run throughout in bridles,
but they stumble before reaching the middle.
18 It has courtyards paved in marble,
and you'd think you are seeing a surface of crystal and a mantle of camphor.
19 A mosaic, encrusted with pearls, and you'd think its floor is musk
whose scent emits a sweet fragrance.
20 Dawn is replaced in it because there arises another daybreak
that shines forth [even] in the deepest dark of night.
21 Lions are silenced in the den of command
in which they turn the ripple of water into a roar.
22 You imagine that pure gold has draped itself over their bodies
and has melted crystal into their mouths,
23 and that lions whose stillness seems to move naturally,
appear as though they found their provocation,
24 while they are recalling their attacks
as they crouch on their hinds ready to pounce.
25 The sun flashes its light and you imagine it as fire,
while its rays appear as lapping tongues.
26 It is as though the swords of the streams have been unsheathed,
now melted without fire and turned into a brook,
27 and as if the gentle breeze has stitched a coat of mail for its water,
and what an exquisite fabric it weaved.
28 With such extraordinary results of creativity
my eyes in its proximity cross toward a river overflowing with wonders:
29 a golden shrubbery that provokes an enchantment
and leaves a profound impression on the mind.
30 They have fashioned the branches in the shape of curved staffs
as though they are hunting birds up above,

31 but want to prevent those birds falling from the branches
from rising up and flying away.
32 You see the beak of each bird
spurting clear water that flows out into streams of silver.
33 Muted, they are counted among the most eloquent,
and when they sing, they whistle their tunes with water.
34 It appears as though there is liquid silver atop every branch
whose [shimmering] threads trickle down,
35 showing you where their drops land in the cistern (pool)
like scattered pearls above the (green) chrysolite.
36 The palace fixtures look down on you with a smile
as though its galaxy of bright stars were a mouthful of teeth,
37 and the doors, plated in solid gold,
are brought into relief with the engraving of their ornaments.
38 Their pegs are studded in gold shaped in perfect globes
that jut out like firm breasts of lovely maidens.
39 The sun removes its diaphanous yellow mantle
that turns the tearful eye away from it.
40 And if you can catch a glimpse of the splendors of its ceiling
you will see a luxuriant garden in the sky.
41 You will be amazed by the gilded swallows
which circle above to build their nests in their towers.
42 The artisans have placed their brushes
with which they paint images of every animal of prey for you to see.
43 It appears as though the sun has a large pot of paint
from which they sketch their ornaments and floral designs.
44 You imagine that in the plaster of the ceiling there is an embroidery
with stripes engraved in lapis lazuli,
45 and embroidered over it is a mantle
that leaves little room for its garment.
46 O king of the earth to whom the King of Heaven
has made you [His] assistant [against] the enemy,
47 how many royal palaces existed before you
and [how many] were persuaded to delay being built after your palaces?

48 You have erected them and you have gained full command,
and from them you have vanquished the enemy!
(Diwan #349: 545–549)

The three poems Ibn Hamdis composed during his stopover at Qal'at Bani Hammad were as much the poet's personal tribute to al-Mansur ibn al-Nasir as they were occasions for him to display his poetic prowess and enhance—and promote—his fame as a court poet in search of a court. However, they are noteworthy in that they lack any allusion to the poet's private angst over life in exile, and they fall far short in enumerating, in grandiose and hyperbolic imagery, the king's qualities, virtues, and feats of righteous rule that he lavished on al-Mu'tamid during his years in Seville. In this, there is, no doubt, a political explanation. Ibn Hamdis was making his way back to Ifriqiya, where the members of his extended family had settled in Sfax, and where the Zirid princes were positioned on the front lines of battle against the Christian forces across the Mediterranean. Having witnessed the rivalries and infighting among the Muslims of al-Andalus, and the wrathful vengeance of the Almoravid forces against the 'Abbadids of Seville, Ibn Hamdis was not about to get caught in the Muslim crossfires. The Hammadids of Qal'at Bani Hammad, after all, had become the bitter rivals of their Zirid cousins in Ifriqiya, who, in turn, were politically and militarily stronger, and thus in a better position to launch counter-offensives against the rising might of the Norman naval forces. Any lavish praise of al-Mansur would undoubtedly draw his intended patrons' unwanted attention.

RETURN TO MAHDIA

Following his departure from Bejaia, Ibn Hamdis arrived to a much changed and frenetic Mahdia. It should be recalled that the half-century reign of Zirid prince al-Mu'izz ibn Badis (r. 1016–1062) had witnessed significant transformations in the central Maghreb, with both dramatic successes and setbacks. The early years saw an expansion of territories that came under his control, a prosperous economy based on wheat production and exports, and a build-up of his military forces. His attempts to settle disputes in the politically riven province of Sicily in 1025 and 1029, as mentioned above, as well as other expeditions he later dispatched, although not successful in achieving their goals, demonstrated, nonetheless, a flexing of Zirid muscle in the Mediterranean Basin. Al-Mu'izz's decision to declare allegiance—even if to only a symbolic effect—to the 'Abbasid caliphate in Baghdad was a rejection of Fatimid Shi'ism that was met enthusiastically by the Sunni Maliki religious establishment and the masses who remined loyal to it.

However, this move came at a cost. As we have seen earlier, the Fatimid rulership in Egypt unleashed hordes of Arabian Banu Hilal and Banu Sulaym tribes who, it should be recalled, had invaded the south of Egypt in search of water and lands to settle. As an act of revenge, the Fatimid caliph al-Mustansir bi-allah (r. 1036–1094) pointed them in the direction of Ifriqiya with enticement of amassing power and wealth. The Hilali invasions had a massive impact of eleventh-century Ifriqiya, among which was forcing both the Zirids and the Hammadids into withdrawing from their capitals of Kairouan and Qal'at Bani Hammad to safer ground in the port cities of Mahdia and Bejaia respectively. In the context of these shifts, one can easily understand the Zirid efforts to build up their navies and look out to the wider Mediterranean.

CONNECTING TO THE ZIRIDS: PRAISE AND BLAME FOR TAMIM

When Ibn Hamdis reached his destination of Ifriqiya, Tamim ibn al-Mu'izz (r. 1062–1108) was ruling from Mahdia. Like his father, his reign lasted a long and difficult half century, with some initial successes followed by a series of disasters, not all of his own making. The realm he inherited was fractured politically and exhausted economically. His failed attempts to rein in the Arabian tribes of the hinterland restricted his control to the cities on the eastern Mediterranean coast, from Sousse (Susa) to Gabes (Qabis). Compounding his troubles were attacks from Pisan and Genoese merchant fleets set on expanding their power base in the Mediterranean. Above all, there were the Normans, now progressing steadily in their conquest of Sicily, to contend with. The thirteenth-century historian Ibn al-Athir (d. 1233) reports that Tamim sent two of his sons, 'Ali and Ayyub, to Sicily soon after his ascension to the throne in 1062 to help negotiate disputes among the three warring warlords. Although the two brothers were warmly received by sundry local factions, they eventually became entangled in disputes that forced them to withdraw from the island, taking back to Mahdia with them their own troops, as well as significant numbers of Muslim Sicilian notables and military personnel.

Ibn Hamdis's return to Ifriqiya after thirteen years in Seville aroused a gamut of emotions for the by-now seasoned expatriate. It brought him back to familiar terrain, in proximity to his family, and in contact with what must have amounted to hundreds, if not thousands, of Muslim refugees fleeing Sicily as a result of the Norman conquest. His return brought him much closer to the theater of what he imagined, or fantasized, was a war of liberation which he had previously envisioned in his verses. Back then, it was only possible to follow Sicily's news from a distance, catching snippets of information from second or third hand reports. His return undoubtedly rekindled emotions over divisiveness, defeat, and loss of homeland that he recently experienced in Seville. His only hope now rested with the Zirid princes and whatever battalions and flotillas they could assemble and dispatch. Tamim, however much he tried, and however well intended he may have been, had to bear some responsibility for the final Norman conquest of Sicily in 1091, but as the most powerful ruler in the central Maghreb, he still needed to be addressed.

Tamim was the fifth Zirid to rule Ifriqiya, and the first of the last four Zirid princes to whom Ibn Hamdis composed his panegyrics. The diwan contains one poem dedicated to him, possibly reflecting the relatively short time Ibn Hamdis's return and resettlement in Ifriqiya overlapped with the last years of Tamim's rule. It may also very well be an indication of the poet's frustration and disappointment with his new patron's failed Sicilian campaigns, emotions, and sentiments he articulates throughout the qasida.

Ibn Hamdis's *Tamim* panegyric contains sixty-two lines and it may be divided, generally speaking, into two segments: a gnomic or existential introduction (lines 1–35); and the praise proper (lines 36–62). The first part collapses themes such as the cruel twists of fate, crying over abandoned encampments, crossing hostile terrain, and growing old. It is most peculiar in that it is voiced in the first person with pronominal referents (*I*, *me*, *my*) present in every line, giving the poem a powerful autobiographical tone, compounded by events documenting the poet's life thus far. Line 35 cursively mentions Tamim as the subject of the praise, and is quickly followed by a seven-line tirade against the poet's Sicilian compatriots for their treacherous infighting. The remainder of the poem, beginning with line 43, returns to the praise proper, but Tamim is addressed in the plural (*humat*: protectors) which may very well be read as addressing all the Zirid princes, kings, and generals. Lines 44–58 comprise a battle scene which may be read as a fictional hypothesis, or perhaps even as a manual of instruction to Tamim on how a battle should be fought. The employment of the present tense, used to indicate not only present action but incomplete action, strongly suggests that the litany of noble qualities and valiant feats of courage are cast in the abstract and yet to be earned:

11 You think that I am forgetting, but I still remember
    the treason of my time and the treason of my companion.
12 [My sword] was nurtured by my character as a young man,
    and its thrashes were aimed only against mine.
13 Many a plant has been overwhelmed by bitterness
    that had once been sweetened by the water of rain clouds.
14 I learned through experience things of which I had been ignorant;
    things are indeed unknown before they are tried.
15 Whoever thought that the waters of deserted wells were sweet,
    discovers upon drinking that his thinking was false.
16 I rode the vast no-man's land on the saddle of many a camel
    that held my ropes as we tore through the desert.
17 Young she-camels, backs arched from emaciation,
    as though they were hands drawing water from the well.
18 When they came upon wells with clear, blue water,
    they surrounded it like eyebrows surround the eyes.

19 Firmly resolved in my hopes, I was made to alight
on the false hope of lifting anxiety from my mind.
20 There is no safe place save in private thoughts,
where I seem to summon everything absent.
21 When I encountered people whose evil was feared,
I avoided them and chose the ascetic's life.
22 I was even fortunate to be visited by a phantom
who repelled every reprover from my bed as I slept.
23 Have the leanness of my body and the whiteness of my forelocks
altered my appearance so that it does not visit?
24 If whosoever is absent counts the months of his exile,
then I have counted eons upon eons for mine.
25 How many a sincere resolution like the swords
has been peeled away by the hands of false hope.
26 I have in the skies of the East a constellation that shines
whenever I reach for its highest stars.
27 I have become so accustomed to my exile from it,
that the string of days has been stacked as if in the palm of the accountant.
28 Whenever Gemini in the sky hears my voice,
it listens to me because of my improvising strange things.
29 How many a soulmate have I in the sky who protects without blame
even the shameful from his enemies.
30 My brother, confidant, I often drank wine with him,
his youth from the hand of time having not been snatched.
31 A fine vintage, [count] how often its long age is mentioned,
from it the paws of the accountants have been filled.
32 When the water wades into the wine's hidden entrails,
pearls appear from it, some floating, some suspended.
33 My evenings in the two Mahdiyya-s were like pearls,
in your world, set upon the neckline.
34 These evenings will not be changed, but will remain as pearls,
strung like necklaces for years on end.
35 If I wanted to glance at the crescent moon,
I would notice Tamim in the firmament of noble qualities.
36 If my country were free, I would go to it with a resolve
that sees separation as a constant affliction.

37 But how can my country be ransomed from captivity,
while it sits in the clutches of the usurping infidels?
38 These dogs have prevailed by devouring my lands,
and after a lull they lunged for the veins.
39 Before my eyes my compatriots succumbed to civil strife,
in which every woodsman lit a bonfire.
40 And their desires for it became such that they conducted themselves
in ways contrary to our faith.
41 Kinfolk showed no mercy to their own people,
as swords dripped with the blood of kin.
42 They were like the joints of the fingers that have been ripped apart,
once held together by the flesh of one hand.
43 Protectors, if you see them in battle,
you would be content just to see the most ferocious lion among them.
44 If they go to fight in the fiercest of battles,
they unleash from their hands thunderbolts in the clouds.
45 On the days when lances clash, they have strong hands
that deliver the lion's liver to the fox in their attack.
46 They have camel stallions that gallop through enemy territory,
whose neighing amplifies the wailing of mourning women,
47 with the camels' ears pointed beneath their swords,
just like the pens of writers made pointed by sharpening.
48 If their ears go around in circles, you would imagine them
striving to hear what is beyond the clouds.
49 If they grow silent in the throes of death, they articulate
with the clang of their swords the flash of their slender sharp edges.
50 You see the flames of fire on the tips of their swords,
and from the hands of swordsmen the enemy are made to taste death.
51 Fear not that these fighters will turn away from death,
[fiercer are they] than lions who retreat to their dens in fear.
52 While some men stray from the path of guidance,
they are guided away from any straying and toward the brightest stars.

53 How many a brave, thoughtful one there are among them,
who attacks from the front and not from behind,
54 and who when he attacks he splits the enemy army in half,
as one would butcher a sheep in a playground.
55 Whenever they attacked the Christians (*Rum*), their entering would be
on the inside of ships, on the backs of sturdy horses;
56 and they would die the death of glory in the thick of battle,
while cowards die in the arms of beautiful women.
57 They [would] stuff pillows with the dust of holy war,
which they will recline upon in their graves;
58 and they would fall like falling stars into the cavity of decline,
and perpetuate the blackness of night on earth.
59 Is there not in God's protection an abode in Noto
upon which the clouds pour forth their abundant rains?
60 I fashion its memory in my mind at every waking moment,
and I draw forth for it the drops of gushing tears.
61 I yearn like the old she-camels for a homeland,
to which the abodes of beautiful maidens are drawing me.
62 Whoever leaves a homeland but whose heart remains in it,
hopes the return of the repentant heart to its body.

(Diwan #27: 28–33)

The closing four lines of this poem are a familiar substitute for the customary prayer to God where Ibn Hamdis pleads for divine intercession to keep the patron safe and strong. They reinforce what is foremost on the poet's mind; that in longing for Sicily, feeling the pangs of guilt for being away from it, and yearning to return, he is composing his panegyric to Tamim to do his duty as 'defender of the faith.'

VIGILANT EYE ON THE NORMAN CONQUEST

Sicily in the decade of the 1060s, as we have seen, was subjected to the chaos caused by the implosion of the Kalbid dynasty and the subsequent division in rulership among the three petty warlords. It was also in this decade when Count Roger, at the invitation of Ibn al-Thumna, it should also be recalled, began his campaign to extend his control over as much Sicilian territory as he could. And across the sea, despite the death in 1062 of al Mui'zz ibn Badis, and the ascension of his son, Tamim ibn al Mu'izz to the throne, Zirid attempts to revive their hegemony and influence over the island of Sicily remained on course. The Zirids had their hands full, fending off the Hilali invasions, while at the same time contending with the Sicilian warlords' political maneuverings in courting alliances with the Fatimids in Egypt. These warlords, for their part, devised strategies to manipulate their traditional North African benefactors with half-hearted claims of allegiance and pleas for support.

Meanwhile, the Normans having already cast their sights on Sicily, were looming large over southern Italy and the central Mediterranean. Robert Guiscard was recently invested as Duke of Apulia by Pope Nicholas II as part of the papal campaign to reclaim Sicily for Christendom. Robert and his younger brother, Roger Borsa, were making inroads into the island while at the same time launching their Apulian campaigns against the resuscitated Byzantine army dispatched by Emperor Constantine X Ducas. The invitation by warlord Ibn al-Thumna came at a fortuitous time for the Normans, and it was, as we have seen, highly advantageous to the Norman advance. Also, in 1062, a significant battle took place in the hilltop fortress of Castrogiovanni (Enna) that ended, with Ibn al-Thumna's help, in a Norman victory. Although Ibn al-Thumna was assassinated soon thereafter, the victory brought a mixed blessing for the Sicilian Muslims in the form of a crude but necessary wake-up call. The two remaining Muslim warlords, along with several minor local Muslim militias, put their differences aside and banded together to hold the Normans restricted to the northeast corner of the island, mostly in Messina and its adjacent regions. The then seven-year-old 'Abd al-Jabbar Ibn Hamdis was still enjoying, if we are to take his verses literally, the idyllic life of a pampered youth in the southeastern province of Val de Noto, and too young to fear, or perhaps shielded from, the ominous signs of Norman invasion.

Despite the political upheavals Sicily continued to enjoy a degree of economic prosperity. The Geniza documents have unearthed a series of letters and bills of sale exposing robust import-export activity that was part of what would eventually be deciphered as a trade triangle among Palermo, Mahdia, and Alexandria that flourished throughout much of the tenth and eleventh centuries. The agricultural sector continued to produce, and the artisans and craftsmen of the urban centers remained actively employed. However much daily life continued on the ground, Muslim Sicily would not be able to withstand much longer either the turmoil brewing from within or the external forces lurking over it from all sides of the Mediterranean. These included the Normans from Apulia and Calabria, a resurgent Byzantium, the Germans to the north, an aggressive crusading papacy, and the Almoravids in the western Maghreb. In January 1072, Robert Guiscard, Duke of Apulia, led a procession as conqueror into Palermo, followed by his brother and numerous Norman knights and noblemen. There he presided over a service of victory celebration at a hastily redesigned cathedral that had been the Grand Mosque of Palermo for the past two centuries. The Norman capture of Trapani in 1077 and Taormina in 1079 secured their occupation of the north and west sections of the island.

The fall of Palermo was a particularly momentous event, and its historical and psychological impact was profound. *Al-Madina*, as Palermo was referred to by Muslim Sicilians, had been the seat of Muslim sovereignty on the island since its capture in 831 when the invading Muslim forces overtook it and expelled the Byzantine patriarch and his government. Since that time, the long line of governors, whether Aghlabid or Fatimid appointees from North Africa, ruled from it, and it became the seat of a resplendent and flourishing Kalbid Court during the second half of the tenth century. Even with the carving up of the island into petty chiefdoms and the emergence of local militias, Palermo represented nonetheless that 'shining city on a hill' for Sicilian Islam.

ODE TO A FALLING HOMELAND

The south and east regions of Sicily remained strongholds of resistance until the fall of Syracuse and the defeat and death of its local ruler,

Ibn 'Abbad, known in Latin sources as Benavert, in 1085. It would be another six years, in 1091, when the remainder of the cities and towns of Noto followed suit in capitulating to the Norman armies. The city of Syracuse and the town of Noto, the abodes of Ibn Hamdis's treasured youth, being among the last strongholds against the Norman conquest, featured more and more prominently in this later stage of his poetry. It is not certain where Ibn Hamdis had actually settled at the precise time these bastions of Muslim resistance fell. A poem he composed as a sermon to his Sicilian compatriots shows that he was monitoring the events closely, and that until the end he clung to his long-held hopes for his beloved homeland's survival. Although history has left us no paper trail regarding how widespread or well-known Ibn Hamdis's poems were to the members of the shrinking community of Muslims on the island, the existence of continuous traffic between the Ifriqiyan mainland and Sicily, not to mention the fact that Ibn Hamdis was addressing them directly in this poem, gives credence to the idea that his voice traveled in their direction:

1 O people of the frontier [of Syracuse], you are not my kinfolk
if you do not do as good Arabs and attack the Barbarians.
2 Do not sleep, for I fear that disasters will crush you
while you dream [false] hopes.
3 How many a cup full to the brim with venom
did the cupbearer serve to the imbiber of the daughter of the vine [wine]!
4 So, direct the faces of your horses towards a battle
that bestows upon the Rum fatherless children and bereaved mothers;
5 [horses] that kick up the dust that dims the daylight of the sun,
just as they did with the stars in the dark of night.
6 In the thick of the gloomy battle clouds, attack with your swords
as if they were flashes of lightning stained red by chopping heads.
7 Let not the swords cease to be drawn from their sheathes,
like rivulets that lie shielded beneath piles of rock.
8 The sword's severing of the head of every infidel
is music to my ears, sweeter than the strumming of the lute.

9 I swear by God! Every one of you is as sharp and penetrating as your swords,
rushing to battle, glimmering with determination,
10 [each one of you] a hero invigorated by plunging himself into the foray,
as though he were yearning for battle, not for peace;
11 [a hero] whose steadfastness sets him on fire,
and this is the ring in his armor that shields him from every thrust and blow;
12 [a hero] who attacks with his weapon concealed,
and when it appears, it breaks out like the dawn from the dark of night,
13 and he plunges it into the [enemy's] body which extracts the soul,
even before the tip exits the flesh,
14 leaving nothing to be ransomed of flesh or blood
except what is left on the bones after they have been stripped.
15 Steadfast, whenever death approaches with jaws wide open,
the rumbling sound of horses throbs repeatedly [like music] to his ears.
16 He has the eyes of the killer lion,
and his heart has the knowledge to turn passivity into action.*
[* A grammatical reference: the heart knows how to conjugate the passive verb.]
17 This is God's country! If you lose its wide open space (*hawa'*)
then your aspirations (*ahwa'*) on earth will be scattered.
18 Your glory will end up in humiliation and exile,
and the unity among you will be obliterated by separation.
19 The land of others is not your land,
nor are its friends and neighbors your friends and neighbors.
20 Can the land of someone else take the place of your land?
Can a milk-less aunt take the place of a mother?
21 O friend, who has connected your love to my love,
just as the second rains connect to the first rains,
22 chain yourself to the country which is your beloved homeland,
and die in your own abode.
23 Never try for even a day to experience exile,
since the mind will never savor the experience of poison.

(Diwan #270: 416–417)

BACK TO THE FAMILY IN SFAX: MOURNING THE LOSS OF AN AUNT AND A WIFE

Ibn Hamdis's return to Ifriqiya reconnected him more closely to his family, in physical proximity and in emotional attachment, but not necessarily in daily contact. Several of his poems, i.e., elegies to relatives recently passed, and epistolary poems of response to his cousin and brother-in-law, Abu al-Hasan 'Ali ibn Yusuf Ibn Abi al-Dar, shed precious light on individual members of his immediate and extended family. As mentioned earlier, 'Abd al-Jabbar was born in Syracuse, in the province of Noto, and suffered the loss of his mother at an early age. Because his father married a young Christian woman soon after her death, it was decided that he and his sister be raised in the house of his paternal grandfather, Muhammad. In keeping with marital customs of that time and place, both brother and sister eventually married their first cousins when they became of marriageable age.

Although we have no exact dating for the family elegies we can estimate that both his aunt and his wife passed away either during the later years of his time in Seville or soon after his departure. Both elegies begin with long and sorrowful gnomic introductions that, in keeping with the poetic conventions of his time, evoke the unjust and devious twists of Fate that eventually hit all its living targets. Both are replete with the essential components of the traditional Arabic elegy, namely, the listing of the laudable qualities of the deceased, and the personal anguish the poet suffers because of his loss. The elegy to his aunt, the woman who was his surrogate mother, died in Sfax, and the news of her death came to him while on the road:

22 Has the cry of one who mourns not reached the people of the East,
  [a cry] that sheds torrents of tears from the lands of the West?
23 May God water a grave that springs in Sfax,
  with streams the soil would prefer to the clouds,
24 to which there extends the veneration of the grave of an aunt,
  whose loss I will lament until my own timc is up;

25 and with tears towards which the sea extends as it floods its shores,
since the sorrow [I feel] makes it flow endlessly.
26 If I felt secure from outpouring, I would increase my flow of tears,
but my fragile heart has taken pity on itself.
27 Against my will, the tongues of passersby announced the sad news.
How do I accept such news from the tongues of travelers?

Ibn Hamdis goes on to emphasize how his aunt's grave in Sfax is not in her homeland: (line 28: "A stranger in a grave, far from the graves of her homeland"), and that she was raised in the noble house of her father, Muhammad, who tilled the Sicilian soil for eighty years. The poet ends his elegy with a direct address to his cousin, the son of the deceased, in which he emphasizes his familial bonds:

49 O, Abu Hasan, our days are jostled against our well-being,
And they are rewarded with affliction and deceived by love.
50 In them I find that your misfortune is my misfortune,
your sadness is my sadness, and your anxieties are mine.
(Diwan #28: 34–37)

The second elegy during this time is addressed to his wife (also, his maternal first cousin). Following a custom (but not a rule) that a man not eulogize his own wife, Ibn Hamdis composed the poem in the first-person voice of his second son, 'Umar who, it should be recalled, was born during the family journey out of Sicily on its way to Sfax. Another curious feature of this poem is that 'Umar, as the implied author of the eulogy, addresses in first-person voice his older brother Abu Bakr:

43 O, Abu Bakr, what has befallen you is indeed overwhelming,
and it makes one cry floods of tears.
44 In love, you are to me a faithful brother,
and my loss belongs to your loss as well.
45 You stand among the finest of noblemen,
through the pure stock of both maternal and paternal uncles.
46 My nature remains akin to your nature through our grief,
and how many an arrow has been borrowed from a sharp sword.
(Diwan #297: 477–480)

These four lines raise a number of intriguing questions. Was Ibn Hamdis projecting onto his second son a respect for his older brother, who may well have been the surrogate head of a family with an absentee father? Might it also give support to the possibility that Abu Bakr had departed for Seville in the company of his father, a common custom of the times when men traveled abroad with their first-born son and, therefore, was himself in need of consolation from the pain of separation and the loss of his mother? Finally, the eulogy mentions in another line the existence of daughters who stood at the bedside of a dying mother in the throes of a fatal illness. The combination of these familial snapshots, i.e., of a eulogizing son addressing his bereft brother over the loss of their mother, and of young women hovering over a seriously ill mother on her deathbed, generated, no doubt, a depth of anguish combined with pangs of guilt that afflicted an absentee father, husband, and nephew long separated from his family.

There are two poems Ibn Hamdis composed to his cousin and brother-in-law, Abu al-Hasan 'Ali, that express more explicitly the conflicting sentiments of a man caught between the obligations to family and the demands of a 'public figure' fighting for a political cause. Abu al-Hasan 'Ali was arguably the closest human being to Ibn Hamdis, being not only linked through blood and marriage, but through a special bonding between two men who grew up together as brothers in the same household. Given the homosocial nature of traditional Arab society, especially among the elite, 'Abd al-Jabbar and Abu al-Hasan 'Ali, cut from the same cloth, shared similar temperaments and life experiences. Both poems, responses to letters written by Abu al-Hasan 'Ali pleading with the itinerant poet to come back and rejoin the family, expose a conscience tormented by feelings of guilt over his familial neglect while, at the same time, experiencing profound frustration and disappointment over Muslim disunity and weakness in the face of Christian advances. One of the poems, and the shorter of the two, implies that it was written in their old age, with both men well over seventy, and may be read as a farewell to the family as Ibn Hamdis comes to terms with his pending mortality and submission to his fate of separation from the family:

I have been yearning for you for sixty long years,
but I was held back by my failings;

16 For those who depart [from place to place] at seventy,
there is the long road of struggle with death;
17 O Abu Hasan, inhale the sweet scent of my farewell,
as though its fragrance is an intoxicating musk.
(Diwan #215: 333–334)

In the longer of the two poems, consisting of thirty-four lines, Ibn Hamdis pours out his soul expressing the pains of separation and exile, blaming in part that existential monster of Fate, but also his own quest for professional fame. The poem captures more forcefully the conflicted feelings of a man caught between personal ambition and family loyalty. It recounts the story of receiving Abu al-Hasan's letter, the mixed joy and anguish he experiences from that, and the excuses he proffers for why his departure has been a difficult but necessary journey for him. The following eight lines extracted from the poem sum up the personal torment, including a reference to the drowning of his beloved slave girl (line 25), that added to the trials and tribulations of the horrendous year of 1091:

5 What is there in perpetual exile
where I see only a full-grown man past the age of youth.
8 Have I not set out to distant lands searching the heights
from where I appeared to be heading toward the stars;
10 O Abu al-Hasan, hear a plea I send to you,
for you still remain dear to me in everlasting companionship.
17 Do not, you all, think of me as having enjoyed myself away from you,
with the merriment of music and a goblet of wine.
24 Have I not mounted my soul in my longing for you
onto the highest of distant mountains awash in greenery?
25 Have I not been among the drowned beckoning with my raised palm
only to be saved by facing my own mortality?
30 You have all in distant lands dispersed in every direction,
like pearls that scattered after falling off their chain;
31 [There is] kin (among you) from whom Fate has restricted my resolve,
and family from whom the Rum dashed my hopes.
(Diwan #282: 432–434)

Having completed three decades of his life as a poet, beginning as a young man celebrating an idyllic youth in his native Sicily, passing through his brief sojourn in North Africa, and culminating in his celebrity as a court poet in Seville, Ibn Hamdis would embark upon the next three decades back in Ifriqiya, lamenting the loss of his youth, mourning the passing of loved ones, and coming to terms with losing forever a homeland.

7

THE POETICS OF JIHAD: AT THE ZIRID COURT IN MAHDIA

Near the end of the first decade of the twelfth century, Ibn Hamdis, now resettled in Ifriqiya and shuttling from the Zirid Court in Mahdia to the family compound in Sfax, composed a qasida to celebrate—or perhaps to bemoan—his fifty-fifth birthday. The poem is fifteen lines long, and its sole theme is that the poet is getting on in years and, as such, is not the man he used to be. The first four lines set the tone of the poem by conjuring the playful image of a limp member that keeps away the young maidens who once graced his verses recalling his real or imagined youth:

1 Five and fifty years have now passed,
and I have contracted an ailment that suffers many a relapse;
2 There is a pair of opposites now inhabiting my body,
a member that is limp, and a posture that remains firm;
3 The lovely young maidens have now turned away from me,
like pug-nosed heifers that guard themselves against the lion;
4 Where there was once wavy hair as black as ink,
there are now white hairs that streak my temples.

(Diwan #166: 282–283)

The poet goes on to reminisce about his carefree days of youth and laments the inevitable process of growing old. He ends the poem with a prayer seeking God's companionship as he, advancing in years, approaches the Day of Judgement.

The death of Tamim ibn al-Mu'izz in 1108 brought his son Yahya ibn Tamim (r. 1108–1115) to the throne. The longevity of the reigns of his grandfather and father, amounting approximately to one century combined, did little to maintain political unity and social cohesion throughout the central Maghreb. However, Yahya, now having reached middle-age, seized the reins of power and worked quickly and efficiently to rebuild Zirid naval power. On the diplomatic front, he made the wise decision to improve relations with both the Fatimids of Egypt and his cousins the Hammadids of Bejaia. Across the sea, there appears to have been something of a cease-fire between the Zirid Court in Mahdia and the Norman Court in Palermo. There is sufficient historical evidence to show that the flow of people and goods between the two 'states' resumed at this time. With all of Sicily now under Norman control, and with Norman assertion of its increasing naval dominance in the central Mediterranean, Yahya proceeded with judicious caution. However, the sores of past mutual enmity and suspicion between Norman Sicily and Muslim Ifriqiya continued to fester.

AT THE COURT OF YAHYA IBN TAMIM

A guardedly optimistic Ibn Hamdis situated himself as closely as possible to the centers of power, and from the scores of panegyrics he composed to Yahya and his son and successor, 'Ali ibn Yahya (r. 1115–1121), it is clear that he enjoyed a position as panegyrist to the Zirid Court. These poems, in the main, addressed historical events of note, such as battles, ascensions to power, and military victories, but they also included messages of greetings and congratulations on the Muslim New Year, the end of Ramadan, or the circumcision of a son. However much Yahya and 'Ali patronized scholarship and the arts at their court, Ibn Hamdis would never find the closeness and bonding he enjoyed at the 'Abbadid Court in Seville, nor would he be surrounded by a vast network of talented poets and accomplished scholars who flourished under al-Mu'tamid's patronage. But the political stakes of being a court poet for the Zirids were much higher, being that Ifriqiya was situated on the front lines with Norman Sicily. In this new political climate, Ibn Hamdis put his best artistic foot forward. He crafted dozens of qasidas, if not of high creativity and lyricism, then of sufficient artistic merit that achieved their goals of projecting images of Zirid political and religious legitimacy. What he could not extol of the virtuous Arab nobility and qualities (*nasab wa hasab*) he weaved throughout his poems to the Arab 'Abbadids, he replaced with the epithet of 'defenders of the faith' onto his praises of the Berber Zirids. This would allow Ibn Hamdis to frame his panegyrics in the context of an Islamic struggle against the infidel enemies, and thus launch his campaign to liberate his homeland of Sicily against the Normans, a theme that dominates much of his poetry henceforth. In a brief and possibly first ode to Yahya, the poet sets a positive note:

1 Sovereignty belongs to you, and the sword that paved the way to your power
    is that with which Islam launched its assault and humiliated the infidels.
2 You stand in the image and likeness of your ancestors, kings,
    and it is as though their fame is musk enhanced in fragrance.
3 All of them deeply rooted in bravery are leaders of men,
    possessing a powerful punch and a piercing plunge.
4 Whoever among them aims himself toward enemy territory with a colossal army,
    and under cover of a dusty sky, leaves it razed to the ground.
5 Due to an accident (*'arad*) of cowardice from their ineptitude [in battle],
    the enemy's true essence (*jawhar*) takes form in the flare-up of war.
6 By destroying their property, you have built a kaaba for noble men
    toward which we steer our ships and camels in pilgrimage.
7 O Son of Tamim, endowed with a glory
    crowned with a sturdy minaret from which can be seen Arcturus, the highest star,
8 one that tells us much about greatness,
    and as much as it tells us we speak of you;
9 you have embarked on reforming the times, so tell us:
    is it justice that governs the realm (*mulk*), or an angel (*malak*) within you?

10 You have rejuvenated what was decaying, and proven right what was wronged,
and you brought close to you one who was afar, and made smile one who cried.

(Diwan #227: 346–347)

Ibn Hamdis's *Yahya* panegyrics are standard fare. Apart from the occasional verses that carry the king's name, these poems would readily apply to any monarch ruling at any time or place in the medieval Muslim world. One familiar feature many of them share is the bipartite structure that includes first a long introduction replicating the form and content of the wine song, and second the praise segment, often of equal length. What stands out prominently in these verses are poetic strategies that Ibn Hamdis will employ: reference to the praised subject in the plural to connect him to all the Zirid rulers; emphasis on the quality of protection and providing a home or safe haven (*ijara wa idafa*), both to the poet personally, and to the implied thousands of Muslims fleeing Sicily; and the repeated epithet of 'defender of the faith' and other Islamic epithets to give the struggle to liberate Sicily the aura and sanctity of a wider Islamic jihad:

22 If a handsome dandy were given a draught of wine to drink,
I would say it was a star that set in the mouth of the moon.
23 He would mix the wine with water from the downpours of rain (generosity),
and give me to drink the residue of what he had consumed.
24 From his goblet there comes together in my mouth
the nectar of the vine, pure rainwater, and the luster of teeth.
25 He [then] sings the praises of Yahya with sweet melodies,
and his kingdom shakes from both sides with rapture.
26 Through al-Mu'izz lil-Din, [Yahya] can boast in glory the best of grandfathers,
and from Tamim the best of fathers.
28 He is a king who stands guard over the frontiers of the Faith,
and who casts aside the enemy with a thunderous army.

———

55 I roamed across the horizons until my exile reached the age of maturity,
    and my education and formation were perfected.
56 And finally I came upon the king,
    the one who extended to me graciously a rope/tent to settle down on this earth.

(Diwan #33: 45–49)

47 O, Son of Tamim, king of our times, and noblest of men,
    you hear the petitions of those who call out to you.
48 Your prosperity flows freely and profusely to all mankind,
    when so much wealth has been a prisoner to greed.
49 In your abode we have settled, one that produces bounty
    and creates a life of luxury to those dying of poverty.
50 Your many resolutions brought us to plunge the depths of the awesome sea,
    like your sharp sword and your lavish favors.

(Diwan #132: 214–218)

REVOLT AND MURDER AT THE ZIRID PALACE

A decade since he returned to Ifriqiya and having established himself as a poet in the service of the Zirid princes, Ibn Hamdis found himself in the midst of a palace coup and an attempted assassination on Yahya to which he succumbed several days later. In the course of the violence, Yahya's chief minister, al-Sharif 'Ali ibn Ahmad al-Fihri, was killed, most likely in his attempt to protect his patron. Al-Fihri bore the name of origin (*nisba*) of 'Sicilian' (*al-Siqilli*), and it is well within the realm of possibility that he was a high-ranking military officer who counted among the throngs of Sicilians emigrating from the island with the Zirid armadas, following the failed attempts to quell the civil unrests of the previous decades. In fact, Ibn Hamdis's diwan contains several poems (panegyrics or elegies) dedicated to Sicilian men of rank, also likely military commanders, i.e., Commander Muhib ibn 'Abd al-Hakam al-Siqilli (Diwan #37: 63–66), Commander 'Abd al-Ghani, and the son of Commander ʻAbd al-ʻAziz al-Siqilli (Diwan #332: 525–529), that show he was in contact with powerful members of the exiled Sicilian community in Ifriqiya serving in either the Zirid government or armed forces.

Ibn Hamdis composed three qasidas on the event: the first is an account of the assassination attempt; the second is an elegy to al-Sharif al-Fihri; and the third is a poem that combines verses of eulogy to Yahya and congratulations to ʻAli ibn Yahya on his ascension to the throne. The first poem reveals the circumstances of the attack, which Ibn Hamdis refers to as an act of 'betrayal.' To dramatize the event, he evokes an incident concerning the attempted poisoning of the Prophet Muhammad by an infidel woman who was taking her revenge against the killing of several of her family members during the Battle of Khaybar:

6 Betrayal, how much of it has filled history since the days of old,
 and how often the epics of its deeds have been told.
7 The weavers of schemes, when they see opportunities,
 resolve to act upon them, and they go for the attack.
8 The Elected One was poisoned by an infidel woman to do him harm,
 as if injury could have affected him at all.
9 With a loud cry and sword in hand,
 he struck the head of the traitors in the early morning.
10 At that time a gang was guided by a darkness of heart,
 and arrogance was their driving force.

(Diwan #133: 218–220)

The poem continues with an extended war song that pits the forces of good against the forces of evil. As he transitions to the praise segment, he mentions the still-alive Yahya by name and compares him to a chameleon, and then cites him as a king of Islam who protects the faith:

22 [He is] like the chameleon that stays high above on its branch,
 when the rays of the sun sizzle with heat.
23 When they saw Yahya, it was his good fortune
 in which victory and success were cast.
24 Since Time is a servant to his dynasty,
 it demolishes his enemy, however numerous they be.

25 He is a king, and for Islam he is its protection,
  an extensive shield that casts a cool shadow.
(Diwan #133: 218-220)

The elegy to al-Sharif al-Fihri is remarkable, by contrast, in its length and the depth of anguish felt by both the poet and, as he states in the poem, the collective *umma* of Muslims. The poem, fifty-seven lines long, commences with an unusually brief two-line gnomic introduction, then proceeds to the eulogy with references to widespread shock and disbelief. The poet follows this with an account of the deceased's funeral procession and the agony of the members of his household, suggesting strongly that the poet was close to al-Fihri and his extended family. The elegy flows through a number of verses that extol his military bravery and accomplishments, then is followed by a litany of [super] human qualities that are at best skimpy in his Zirid panegyrics by comparison. In line 26, he refers to al-Fihri as "a faithful advisor to the king, whose judgement was flawless," and describes him as "astute, merciful, of noble origin, devoid of obscene speech and evil deeds, never breaking promises or denying one in need of assistance." He praises him, above all, as a hero who died a martyr.

The third poem for this occasion is the combined elegy-praise. The suddenness and shock of these events would warrant such a combination, but the discordant mixture of deep sorrow and celebratory joy throughout the poem is highly unusual. Yet into this curious meshing of opposite moods we read the politics of the times.

1 Hardly is one sword sheathed when another one is drawn,
  when one moon disappears only to have another one rise.
2 Yahya is deceased, and the people have died with him,
  until 'Ali came upon them, and lo, they are revived.
3 They are now resurrected with joy upon his ascension to the throne,
  after having been laid to rest in grief from Yahya's demise.
4 'Ali has taken the oath and the teeth of the realm are grinning,
  while on account of the father floods of tears fill their eyes.
(Diwan #134: 221-223)

Yahya's short reign came after his father's half-century, making him, as was mentioned above, a man in his mature-to-ageing years. His policies of reaching out, or accommodation, to nemeses, must have made him look weak, at least in the eyes of Ibn Hamdis and other Sicilian exiles of Ifriqiya. The treaties and agreements Yahya concluded with the Norman Court of Roger II, as much as they were the products of a realpolitik of the place and times, undoubtedly added further meaning to Ibn Hamdis's repeated accusations of 'betrayal' throughout his poems. While his firebrand poetics had taken on a jihadist spirit, especially in his praise and elegy qasida[s], Ibn Hamdis was by now sufficiently battled-tested and politically astute to walk the precarious tightrope that dangled between internal and external complexities, as this third qasida in all its politically measured tone shows. It was increasingly evident that the Normans, at the time of Yahya's death and 'Ali ibn Yahya's assumption to power in 1115, held the upper hand in the central Mediterranean, and their North African campaigns were working to their advantage. King Roger succeeded in establishing embassies and merchant communities in several North African towns, and he reaped vast profits in trading Sicilian wheat to his Muslim neighbors when they suffered the consequences of a depleted agrarian economy, and bartering to his benefit for North African gold. In addition to struggling to circumvent Norman advances along the central North African coast to their advantage, the Zirids continued to be plagued by internal disputes of which the Arab-rallying, Muslim-unifying Ibn Hamdis was so painfully aware.

BREAKING RANKS IN GABES

A case in point is graphically illustrated in the persona of Rafi' ibn Makan, local governor of Gabes. Wishing to expand both his power and wealth from the lucrative trade routes along the southern coast of Ifriqiya, Rafi' had a massive ship built to achieve his goals. His project actually began under the reign of Yahya, who seems to have turned a blind eye to his ambitions. However, when 'Ali acceded to the throne, he saw this as a brazen challenge to his authority, and quickly dispatched a flotilla to seize and confiscate the ship. Rafi' responded by contacting the Normans for help, and King Roger was only too happy to comply. Roger commanded his admiral and chief vizier, the brilliant, charismatic, ambitious, and duplicitous George of Antioch, a political refugee from Byzantine Syria who had once made his way to the upper levels of Tamim's government, only to defect to the Normans, to lead the fleet to assist the rebellious Rafi'. 'Ali, in a show of force, stood his ground and scored a victory. He expelled Rafi' from Gabes and arrested numerous Norman merchants, thus earning for himself at once the wrath of King Roger and the exuberant verses of praise from a hopeful Ibn Hamdis:

38 It is because of you that the religion of the Muslims
enjoys victory over the religion of the Christians.
39 You protected its [Islam's] sanctity, by land and by sea,
with a whetted sword by which perdition sustains itself.
40 God has granted you good judgement in dealing with the infidels,
the cause of which they suffered humiliation and defeat.
41 They saw a warship that spewed petroleum,
that when ignited would extinguish their souls.
42 It was as though the liquid pitch inside the tubes
flowed from it in order to roast their faces.
43 When the neck of the infidel was snapped by him,
there arose a howling bellow of death.
44 It was as if the bubbling [of lava] from the volcano inside the ship
made you envision the terrors of hell,
45 bronze-like in color, from which blazes were emitted,
wreaking havoc on the spirits of the infidel.

(Diwan #138: 236–240)

FROM SEVILLE TO NICOTERA AND MAHDIA: THE ALMORAVIDS MOVE EAST

As much as these events at Gabes, exquisitely narrated by Ibn Hamdis with graphic images of Greek fire employed at the time, and consonant with contemporaneous historical accounts to that effect, made a hero out of 'Ali ibn Yahya, it exacerbated the chaos of Ifriqiya and turned the coastal cities stretching from Mahdia to Gabes into war zones. Roger II's naval forces, not to mention those of Pisa and Genoa, increased their forays into porous areas along the coast as well as to the interior, meddling in internal affairs, flexing their military and economic muscles, and forging alliances with dissident Arab and Berber tribes, while the tribes themselves continued their rivalries for power among themselves. Ibn Hamdis found himself once again in a situation uncannily reminiscent of his later years in Seville. The Zirid 'Ali, like the 'Abbadid al-Mu'tamid, was ruling over a shrinking kingdom caught between the relentless attempts of local warlords to wrest as much territory as they could, and rapacious Christian campaigns aimed at controlling as much of Muslim-held territory as they could. 'Ali, facing the realities of new power dynamics in a rapidly shifting Mediterranean, needed bigger guns to protect his realm. The Fatimids of Egypt, while facing more and more toward points East, were preoccupied with their own internal challenges, and the Hammadids of Bejaia, themselves taking advantage of peaceful relations with the Normans, were too remote and often at odds with the Zirid Court. The logical solution for 'Ali was to be found, as was the case of al-Mu'tamid thirty years ago, in the Almoravids.

Given the absence of any written record other than verses from Ibn Hamdis's panegyrics and elegies that are, once again, carefully measured to maintain as much political neutrality toward intra-Muslim divisiveness, we can only imagine the poet's ambivalence with regard to the Almoravids. After all, it was Yusuf ibn Tashufin and his army of nomadic warriors who rode into Seville and set fire to the 'Abbadid kingdom, sending al-Mu'tamid and the surviving members of his family into a humiliating exile in 1091. On the other hand, they were largely responsible for defeating Alfonso VI at the Battle of Zallaqa, it should be recalled, putting a roadblock in the path of the Christian conquests in Spain. But by 1106, with the death of Yusuf, his son, 'Ali ibn Yusuf ibn Tashufin (r. 1106–1143), inherited the Almoravid throne. Born in the city of Sabta (modern Ceuta) and having lived in al-Andalus, 'Ali was raised in an urban environment and did not inherit his father's rugged nomadic sensibilities nor his austere religious and political views. Also, Ibn Hamdis's life experiences and his acute observations on the twists of fate and the political machinations of his time rendered him a realist. In his lifelong goal to liberate his beloved homeland of Sicily, he saw in the Almoravids his best hope.

After all, the Almoravids, in addition to putting an effective end to the petty kingdoms and principalities among the Muslims of al-Andalus, succeeded as well in establishing something of a unified 'state' throughout the western Maghreb by way of suppressing local rivalries among the tribes and forging strong ties with the Sunni Maliki clerics and scholars that put into place a significant degree of religio-cultural unity throughout much of their realm. As Ibn Hamdis sang the praises of the Zirids, Yahya, 'Ali, and the soon to come al-Hasan, he undoubtedly had 'Ali ibn Yusuf ibn Tashufin somewhere in mind.

Roger II's willingness to aid the treasonous Rafi' ibn Makan of Gabes brought Norman-Zirid relations to a dangerous low, and 'Ali ibn Yahya's appeal to the Almoravids went further in triggering both sides to set off rounds of threats of mobilizing for war. Hostilities erupted when in 1122–1123, the Almoravid navy launched a surprise attack on the Calabrian port city of Nicotera, some fifty miles north of Messina, killing a significant number of soldiers and taking scores of women and children as slaves. The attack, a clear display of Almoravid military might and demonstration of their advancement from the western to the central Mediterranean, bore the fingerprints, at least in the eyes of Roger II and his commanding officers, of 'Ali ibn Yahya at Mahdia. In the summer of the following year, the battle lines were drawn and a full-fledged war broke out on a small island, *Jazirat al-Ahasi*, ten miles off the coast of Mahdia. Much of the fighting took place in and around an ancient but well-fortified castle overlooking the sea. As I have written elsewhere, the castle, referred to by the Arab historians as *al-Dimas*, was the site of centuries of contestation over military and mercantile domination of the central Mediterranean [Granara, 2012]. The battle ended in a surprise Zirid victory over the Normans, and it was lavishly celebrated in verse by Ibn Hamdis.

VICTORY AT AL-DIMAS

Al-Hasan ibn 'Ali ibn Yahya ibn Tamim, the eighth and last Zirid prince to rule Ifriqiya, was the subject and recipient of Ibn Hamdis's congratulatory ode which the poet composed and delivered following the victory at al-Dimas in 1123. Al-Hasan was a mere thirteen-year-old who had fallen onto the throne two years earlier with the sudden death of his father, 'Ali, who was the actual architect and victor of this battle. It was 'Ali's military build-up, his steadfast defiance against the Normans, his alliance with the Arab tribes in the central Maghreb, and his reaching out to the Almoravids that in combination brought about this victory. The septuagenarian Ibn Hamdis was at least cautiously ecstatic, and his 75-line poem was devoted to recounting the details of the battle and preserving his account of the victory for perpetuity. There is no customary gnomic introduction bemoaning Fate's heavy hand in human events. The description of the battle, from events leading up to its outbreak to the listing of names and places involved, provides a documentarity that reads faithfully to the Arabic chronicles. The artistry of the poem rests on a playful mixture of praise and invective expressed in both *jahili* and Islamic poetic tropes and imagery, bouncing back and forth from the bravery of the victor to the cowardice of the vanquished, pitting the glory of Islam as true faith against the infamy of [Christian] infidelity. The following lines extracted from the poem capture vividly the praise/invective binary:

12 The red of their blood is like the wine they pour;
and from it the points of their lush green swords turned crimson.
13 The pale-faced (Normans) have faces that turn yellow out of fear;
and their hands, from all that they ask for, remain bare.
14 When they call to arms, they spread out like flocks of sand grouse,
in every distant land you may find them [fleeing] in flight.

———

24 Ask about them at [the battle of] Dimas and you will hear their story,
of how on this islet they were butchered by well-honed spears.
25 They took for booty only hopes that deceived them,
and in the castle, they got very little for the taking.

———

61 The Arabs launched a jihad against the ʻAjam,
like brave lions launching their war against a herd of swine.

———

64 Squadrons from every tribe came forth to perform his duty of jihad;
there is no pardon for whoever neglects it.
65 Through them, God has strengthened Muhammad's religion,
and His divine providence added protection to them.
66 To the last sword the tribes chased away the enemy,
giving new life to both flatlands and rocky terrain.
68 [Hasan] Ibn ʻAli has protected the [sacred] land of Islam;
like the lion attacking with both claws but only receiving a scratch.

(Diwan #143: 252–257)

The Muslim victory at Dimas would resurface sporadically in later verses in Ibn Hamdis's diwan. However, it did not stop the tidal wave of Norman advances in North Africa. As the Zirid dynasty grew weaker under al-Hasan's rule, and the cities of the Ifriqiyan coast, from Mahdia, Sfax, Gabes and the island of Jerba, staggered in and out of Norman control, Ibn Hamdis's hopes for Muslim Sicily's liberation were steadily dashing. Also, while most of the petty kingdoms and principalities of Muslim Spain were slipping away from Almoravid control, as much the result of the Christian advances as the rising tides of the Almohad movement, Ibn Hamdis would find it most difficult to extol either the Almoravids, or the Zirids, as 'defenders of the faith' with much credibility.

THE ALMOHADS ON THE HORIZON

Abu ʻAbd Allah Muhammad Ibn Tumart, a Berber from the Masmuda tribe of the Zanata confederation from southern Morocco, was a religious scholar and puritanical reformer who began his rebellion against the Almoravids in 1125. Almohad appeal was based on exploiting the failure of the Almoravids to push back against Christian advances, and it benefitted as well from propagating a platform of religious purification and reform that gained wide popular support, especially among the Berber tribes throughout North Africa. When Ibn Tumart died in 1130, he was succeeded by 'Abd al-Mu'min ibn 'Ali al-Kumi, a strong and charismatic leader who not only succeeded in stalling the Christian conquest in Spain, but who eventually directed his massive forces to the central Maghreb where he expanded the sphere of his power and influence. To project forward, in the year 1148, fifteen years after Ibn Hamdis's death, Zirid prince al-Hasan ibn 'Ali surrendered to the Norman fleet commanded by George of Antioch, and handed Mahdia over to the Norman Sicilians, putting an end to the 175-year reign of the Zirid dynasty in Ifriqiya. In that same year, the Almohads put an effective end to the century-long rule of the Almoravids.

In spite of the fact that both of these events occurred after the passing of Ibn Hamdis, they were highly significant as posthumous closures to the exiled Sicilian poet's life story. Given that he spent nearly forty years of his life composing and performing his poetry in the service of the Zirid princes in the hopes that their efforts to resist the Norman occupation of Sicily would liberate his homeland and bring him home, he would have responded to these events with mixed emotions. It would not be until the year 1160 when the Normans surrendered to the Almohads all of their territories they captured and controlled in the Maghreb in return for safe passage back to Sicily. With that dash of fleeting hope from al-Dimas having long dissipated into the cruel twists of fate, Ibn Hamdis would very well have found solace in the words of the Almohad historian al-Marakushi: "Through him ['Abd al-Mu'min] God stamped out *kufr* in Ifriqiya."

8

TIME OF REFLECTION: ASCETIC VERSES AND ARABS AT THE NORMAN COURT

By the end of the year 1123, Ibn Hamdis, reaching the age of seventy, entered the last decade of his life. With the victory of al-Dimas now behind him, the Normans of Sicily continued their North African campaigns with staggering success as Zirid prince al-Hasan ibn ʻAli fought a series of valiant but losing battles against them. Ibn Hamdis, ever the loyal court poet, penned several more panegyrics to him, but the fire of his panegyrics was losing its light and heat. At this time, the elderly ʻAbd al-Jabbar took to composing short poems, labeled in his diwan as *zuhdiyyat* (singular: *zuhdiyya*).

RETREAT INTO DEVOTIONAL VERSE

The *zuhdiyya* is best described as a pious, homiletic, or ascetic poem that came into its own as a literary genre by the early ninth century. It traces its poetic roots to the pre-Islamic classical qasida where its verses were most prominent in the gnomic introductions, especially in elegies. Its themes included the finiteness of life, man's mortality, and the cruel and unjust twists of Fate. Like the love song, the wine song, and the battle song, this devotional poem broke out from its role as a sub-theme in the tripartite qasida and developed as a free-standing poetic genre in the post-Islamic period, often adopting devotional Islamic language and images. Its name is derived from the root- z-h-d, denoting 'renunciation,' and it connotes the evolved meanings of 'abstinence' and/or 'asceticism.' Less significant in strictly theological or legal contexts, the abstract noun (*zuhd*) or the active participle (*zaahid*) took on broader religious, political, and social significations throughout the early centuries of Islam. In Ibn Hamdis's time and place, the epithet of the *zaahid* would be applied, often but not exclusively, to a cleric, scholar, or writer who rejected the comforts and wealth of a [decadent] life, or an individual who rejected political patronage, withdrew from the trappings of the material world to a life in seclusion and, in more graphic images, lived a simple life of extremely modest dress and nourishment, all with the aim of devoting one's life exclusively to God. In literature, the *zuhdiyya* often overlapped with the sermon (*wa'z*), whereupon it carried the messages of exhortation and calls for repentance (*tawba*), as shown in the following Ibn Hamdis poem:

1 You have been warned by your graying side curls
as well as by the loss of your fleeting youth.
2 For seventy years you have seen the sun,
with your own two eyes, rising and setting.
3 Woe unto thee! Has one moment passed
when your soul has been repulsed by error?
4 You gave yourself over to doing what has not preserved you,
as though you were a conniving temptress.
5 Your [earthly] world enticed you
when it entrusted you with its deceptive hopes.
6 Did you imagine it as a friend?
Surely, by its events it was a miserable companion!
7 Has it not stripped the cloak of youth from you?
Does something stolen ever get returned?
8 Verily, every moment of time
eats away and swallows up your life.
9 And then death, from its part,
pounces on you with its outstretched claws.
10 Have you not seen it with the stones of ruination,
for every scorching heat has a hurricane.

11 [It is] as though your soul had a magnet
by which it was drawn to evil deeds.
12 O you, whose sin is ever present
and whose remorse is nowhere to be found,
13 dissolve from yourself a heart with which you compete
with the competitors of your gushing tears.
14 On account of all the sins committed in youth,
the angels who record our deeds have grown exhausted.
15 May God withhold His punishment from you,
for if not, then the consequences will be abominable.
(Diwan #30: 40–41)

The *zuhdiyya* poems of the elderly Ibn Hamdis do not espouse a complete withdrawal from the world, nor do they articulate deeply religious or liturgical sentiments. They bear no signs of advocating the physical jihad that had been permeating his panegyrics and elegies since his arrival at the Zirid Court, nor do they bear much resemblance to Sufi mystical poetry that was on the rise throughout the Muslim world at the time. Ibn Hamdis's predilection for the *zuhdiyya* at this time of his life and career was the result of several factors. First, it was the natural response of a man growing old and facing his own mortality. The mood was one of heightened introspection and meditation on his own life as well as on the human condition. His *zuhd* poems were infused with references to a weakened body, whitened hair, and bodily ailments brought on by the ravages of Time. Second, his 'devotional poems' were both confessional and repentant. They harp on past sins and misdeeds, with a cautious eye, no doubt, on his pending death, the Day of Judgement, and his life in the hereafter. In that, God takes on greater agency as the just and powerful replacement of the deceitful *jahili* Fate. God appears more of a merciful confessor to whom the poet must 'confess his sins.' If we take into account the written record of his lived experiences, that is, the vast corpus of his poetry, we can imagine that he may have been reflecting on his many profane verses of 'wine, women, and song' composed on occasions which a newly pious man would in old age deem as decadent and sinful. His sins may also be attributed to a life largely devoted to art and politics which distracted him from religious duties. We have no record of Ibn Hamdis ever having made his pilgrimage to Mecca, and one wonders if he prayed five times a day, kept the Ramadan fast, or gave alms to the poor. And third, Ibn Hamdis's *zuhdiyya* is inspired by, or haunted by, his own long life of exile. Did his late-life contemplation and its catalogue of sins include his choice to leave Sicily, his failure to return, or his absence as a father, husband, brother, and uncle?

Both the thematic and artistic connections between the *zuhdiyya* and his previous worldly political poems hinge on his coming to terms with his exile. The abandonment of ancient abodes, the departure or separation from the beloved, the crossing of hostile terrains, the praises and pleas to all those who held the reins of power and provided a safe haven and a helping hand were inscribed into his hundreds of poems that recorded a life lived far from the beloved homeland, on the road, and at the mercy of the patronage and generosity of strangers throughout his constant longing to return. These devotional poems, penned late in life, were inspired by the reality of an exile and a festering sense of estrangement that were the offspring of the cruel and deceptive hand of Fate compounded by the haunting memory of the poet's own sins. With the fleeting victory of al-Dimas juggling his memory, Sicily the beloved homeland, a landscape for the innocent pleasures of an idyllic youth, and Islam's proud frontier where brave forefathers battled the enemy, tilled the soil, and rested in eternal peace, was looming larger as an abandoned campsite, a defeated abode, a paradise lost, and the mirror of his conscience. Cherished memories, real or imagined, turned into pangs of guilt and cause for repentance. The Sicily of his ascetic verses composed in old age evolved into a larger metaphor for the realities of loss, estrangement, and above all, betrayal. Where Ibn Hamdis once fashioned images of the villains as barbaric and uncouth unbelievers (*'ilj* pl. *'uluj*) who pillaged and stole the land of Muslims, or even as fractious and treasonous compatriots who "succumbed to civil strife, in which every woodsman lit a bonfire," the poet came to see the villain as traitors of a different sort; all those who abandoned the homeland or failed to liberate it. His ascetic poems of late life, as I have been arguing, point the finger at himself.

ARABS AND MUSLIM CULTURE AT THE NORMAN COURT IN PALERMO

One of the great ironies of Muslim Sicilian history is that Arabic culture on the island came into full bloom during a period that spanned the second half of the eleventh century and the first half of the twelfth century, that is, during the years of Norman invasion and the first decades of Roger II's rule. Much of the credit for this is in the timing: it took over a century following the Muslim conquest that began in 827 for Muslim Sicilian society to develop beyond a primarily military one. With the rise and expansion of urban centers, population growth and immigration, and the expansion of trade, farming, industry, and education, Muslim Sicily gradually evolved to include many aspects of a 'civil' society. Despite the frequent outburst of factionalism that plagued and challenged the political and social cohesion of the island, the religious, linguistic, and cultural seeds of what I have been referring to as the 'spiritual' jihad sprouted in time, and it was to Roger's great benefit to reap the harvest of what had been sown long ago.

Credit is due as well to the first Norman rulers, Roger II above all, for their high-profile patronage of Muslim scholars, and their revival of Islamic art and architecture, much of which had perished in the violence of the later decades of the eleventh century. When the thirteenth-century historian Ibn al-Athir composed his account of the downfall of Muslim Sicily, he ended it with a brief description of Roger II's ascendency as ruler of the island, stating that:

> he followed the customs of Muslim rulers, kept in place [Muslim] positions and other governing structures, and established a court of grievances that protected the rights of all citizens, winning, whereby, the loyalty and affection of the island's Muslim population.
>
> (BAS 35: 278)

The passage projects a stark contrast to the numerous images Ibn Hamdis and other exiled Sicilian poets projected of their Norman nemesis; that is, of a brutish infidel tyrant who usurped the beloved homeland and became the enemy of Islam and Muslims. Roger ascended the throne upon the death of his father, Roger Borsa I, in

1095 as a ten-year-old, only four years after Ibn Hamdis returned from Seville. After a period of regency under his mother, Adelaide del Vasto, daughter of a prominent Ligurian nobleman, he assumed actual power as Count Roger in 1112, and was later coronated as King Roger by papal bull on Christmas Day in 1130. His reign overlapped, it should be recalled, with the reigns of the last three Zirid princes: Yahya, ʻAli, and al-Hasan. Ironically, while Ibn Hamdis was composing his invectives against him, Count/King Roger was presiding over a burgeoning court that attracted and patronized Arab scholars, physicians, and poets and, at the same time, was forging alliances and enacting peace treaties with the Zirid princes, as well as other petty princes and tribal warlords across the Mediterranean. The fact that the young Roger's first wife was Elvira of Castille, the daughter of Alfonso VI, the long-time nemesis of his former beloved patron, al-Muʻtamid of Seville, did nothing to soften the vitriol his verses spewed on his leading poetic villain.

What indeed exacerbated Ibn Hamdis's rage against deceit and betrayal was that the Sicily of Roger II, notwithstanding the waves of emigration that occurred during the last decades of the eleventh century, continued to be home to a substantial number of Muslims who continued to live their lives with varying degrees of status and security. Many participated in public life as farmers, craftsmen, and merchants; others enjoyed the security of military or civilian employment under the new government with court protection. The 'palace Saracens,' eunuchs who may or may not have been forced to convert to Christianity, as well as scribes, accountants, translators, and other skilled laborers, not to mention the many slaves of various categories and ranks, were all brought into the system in ways that replicated previous Muslim practices. The new circumstances in which most Muslims found themselves as a minority constituted, in effect, a kind of *dhimmi* status that was all too familiar to Muslims.

Given that Ibn Hamdis lived and breathed Arabic poetry all of his long life, it must have been especially disturbing for him to know that Roger II was the heroic subject of panegyrics composed in the same language, idiom, and traditions of his beloved classical Arabic qasida. The Sicilian-Arabic literary archive has bequeathed to us hundreds of verses penned by Arab Muslims during the years of Roger II's reign, i.e., from 1112 to 1154. Unfortunately, much of this poetry has survived in fragments plucked from later anthologies that aimed to catalogue the names of poets along with selections of their best work. Also, the archive provides ample information that many anthologists chose to delete or 'bowdlerize' verses from numerous Sicilian panegyrics to Roger as unfit to publish, being that they sang the praises of the enemy infidel. Three examples, briefly sketched below, illustrate the range and tenor of Roger's Arabic panegyrics and provide fleeting snapshots of Arabic cultural life in twelfth century Norman Sicily:

'Abd al-Rahman ibn Muhammad ibn 'Umar al-Buthayri [*Mu'jam* #60: 58–9] from the city of Buthayra (modern Butera), was a scholar of Quran sciences and the epistolary arts (i.e., official correspondence, diplomatics, essays, and expository prose), most likely having being trained as a scribe in government service. There remain twelve lines of a poem he composed in praise of Roger II, the bulk of which is dedicated to extolling the king's architectural accomplishments. The four lines at the beginning of the poem comprise a wine song replete with the familiar tropes of passing the goblet from imbiber to imbiber, keeping beat to accompanying music and, most conducive to my thesis, staking claim to Sicily as (paradisiacal) abode. The remaining eight lines focus on descriptions of Roger's palaces, including gardens, loggias and fountains; Abu Hafs 'Umar ibn Hasan [*Mu'jam* #99:149–50] was a reputable Sicilian philologist and grammarian. His extant verses to Roger take the form of a love poem in which the poet/lover is rejected by the beloved. Abu Hafs's incarceration and the intertextuality with a poem dedicated to the Prophet would undoubtedly win over an Arabic-speaking or Arabic-reading audience's sympathy. The poem's attributes of generosity, courage, and supernatural prowess, resonating as much with *jahili* tropes as they do with post-Islam poetics, imply a contractual bond whereby the poet sells his praises to the patron for a reward. We have the comment of the anthologist editing the poem concerning praising the infidel, offering excuses that Abu Hafs is writing his verses under duress, and should not be held to blame for it; Abu al-Daw' Siraj ibn Ahmad ibn Raja' [*Mu'jam* #44: 43–44] was a professional scribe, cited as being a 'keen observer, sharp witted, and creative and refined in the manner in which he composes his verses.' He was the son of a professional scribe and likely an employee of the Norman court as well. Jeremy Johns describes him as a member of a 'distinguished Palermitan family which provided the qadi posting (chief judgeship) of Palermo in three successive generations' [Johns: 88]. The three poems whose extracts survive in his biography include: a poem of response to a request for a loan of a book by a jurist; a poem in the form of a love song that treats trachoma; and an elegy composed on the death of one of Roger II's sons. The scant information in the biography provides a brief but illuminating picture of the ties that bound members of this dwindling community of Arab intellectuals in what remained of Muslim Sicily, as illustrated in the content of the first two poems. What survives of the elegy amounts to seventeen lines that, despite the appearance of editorial deletions, display a remarkable thematic cohesion. Historical accounts report that Roger lost several sons, both young and matured, but several lines that evoke tents, swords, and horses in a state of mourning suggest that the eulogized was a young man who was serving in his father's army.

These verses, along with the remains of the two other poems cited in the biography, demonstrate Abu al-Daw's considerable talent and creativity in the use of the poetic conventions of antithesis and paronomasia that were hallmarks of neoclassical Arabic poetry in those times. And keeping with literary tradition, the poem begins with the customary brooding and aphoristic statements common to classical poetry. The point to be emphasized here is that Arabic poetry, in all its classical features, was alive and well in Roger II's Sicily. The poet then continues by casting the masses as the anguished lovers of the Arabic *ghazal* waning from the loss of the beloved. The poem's last five surviving lines conjure images of doom in the tradition of Arab-Islamic apocalyptic legends: the reversal of the natural order (i.e., children's hair turning gray), the appearance of a harbinger who summons the masses; and throngs tearing out their own hearts instead of the more familiar rending their clothing.

However much an audience listening to these verses would understand and accept them, in all their artistic hyperbole, as poetic speech appropriate to the elegiac occasion, the ominous warnings of a world coming to an end would resonate more forcefully with the Muslim community, especially at a time when Arabic and Muslim culture was losing ground against the tide of demographic and political changes sweeping the island. The influx of the Lombards and other Christian groups coming from the Italian mainland and their hostility toward the Muslims, along with the sharp rhetoric promoted by the Papacy for reconquest of lands held by the Muslims, created what Alex Metcalfe describes as 'the long-term malaise and brewing discontent in the Muslim community' [Metcalfe: 276]. The ambiguity of these apocalyptic verses aside, these extant verses in praise of Roger II demonstrate once again how the classical Arabic qasida, Bedouin and pagan in world view, survived the transition to Islam, and was capable, as I have argued elsewhere [Granara, 2019], of reconciling itself to a new historical consciousness and a radically different system of beliefs and practices. The fact that the Arabs of Norman Sicily in the twelfth century could compose panegyrics to an infidel king, while adhering faithfully to the conventions of literary traditions spawned in the deserts of the Arabian Peninsula centuries before and, at the same time, maintaining local interest, worldly relevance, and artistic credibility with their audience, undoubtedly shook Ibn Hamdis to his core.

Several months before Roger II died in 1154, and twenty years after the passing of Ibn Hamdis, the Christian Norman king of the poet's beloved homeland was presented with a book by famed geographer al-Idrisi (1099–1160). The scion of a noble Arab family with roots in Muslim Spain (al-Andalus), Muhammad ibn Muhammad ibn al-Idrisi traced his ancestry to the Hammudid family of Malaga, a family which, like Ibn Hamdis's, encountered its own experiences of exile during periods of Muslim political upheavals of the eleventh century. His book on world geography, commissioned by King Roger, was entitled *Kitab Nuzhat al-Mushtaq fi ikhtiraq al-Afaq* (The Excursion of One Longing to Cross the Horizons), and was accompanied by a map of the world inscribed on a massive disc of solid silver. Ibn Hamdis did not live to witness or hear about this momentous occasion, but he most likely knew about al-Idrisi, given his penchant to monitor events of Sicily from wherever he alighted. Like the poets mentioned above, al-Idrisi, in his Introduction to what is now referred to as his *Kitab*

Rujar (The Book of Roger), composed a litany of virtues he attributed to the grandeur of the Norman King of Sicily.

Ibn Hamdis was a man totally committed to the written word, to the power and majesty of Arabic poetry, and devoted to the rich literary heritage of the Arabs and the moral fortitude of the Islamic faith. In his long life he witnessed the momentous events of history and he developed, along the way, an acute historical consciousness that allowed him to study human history, from the ancients to his own turbulent times. Ibn Hamdis no doubt fully appreciated the impact the Arabic panegyrics would have on the legacy of Roger II, the man who, in his view, stood in the way of Sicily's return to *Dar al-Islam*, the abandoned abode of lovers, the paradise of his idyllic youth, and the 'covert for gazelles.' In penning his poems in the last years of his life, his villains of deceit and the perpetrators of treason and betrayal were those who accepted defeat, contributed to and flourished in an infidel society, and above all lauded the enemy in verse.

9

TWILIGHT: BLINDNESS, LOSS, AND DEFEAT

By the third decade of the twelfth century, and some sixty years since departing from Syracuse, 'Abd al-Jabbar Ibn Hamdis was finally coming to terms with his lot in life as he faced his imminent demise. His was a life spent much on the road. The arduous journeys on horseback crossing hostile terrains, by land and by sea, the forays into and around battlefields to witness and document wars and skirmishes with enemies and rivals, his numerous attempts to cultivate connections and forge alliances with warring tribes, shuffling around tents, palaces, and corridors of power trying to keep his head above the political intrigues and backbiting that plagued the world of medieval Muslim politics, and the death of loved ones, all took their toll on the itinerant poet-in-exile. As he approached his eightieth birthday, Ibn Hamdis suffered the trials and tribulations of a weakened and dysfunctional body. Following his natural inclinations, and relying on his well-honed professional craft, he chose to express himself in verse:

1 I have a walking stick which I praise by way of humiliation
and with which I go forth as my foot drags behind.
2 Whenever I hold onto it, I am delighted
not by what I gained [in life], but by my life of eighty years.
3 It is as if I am the archer's bow and it is its string,
and I shoot my arrows with the shot of a gray-haired old man.

(Diwan #300: 482)

LOSING SIGHT

This short poem reveals a sharpness of mind and a still-powerful poetic instinct that allowed Ibn Hamdis to poke fun at himself, especially on matters that pertained to his own body that was subjected to the universal laws of nature. His earlier pieces complaining of bedbugs or discovering the horrors of a first gray hair also displayed a penchant for humor by way of short poems, almost limerick-like in their effect. But on more serious matters, Ibn Hamdis was never light or playful. Having for so long crossed the vast swathes of arid desert with dry air and dust storms, and having traversed the seas under stormy wintry conditions, he succumbed to trachoma that left him blind. Ibn Hamdis composed several poems touching on this and other ophthalmic diseases, a recurring theme in medieval Arabic poetry which would indicate that it was a malady suffered by many at that time. The following poem carries a somber tone, one the poet used to describe his suffering with clusters of images that resonate with love poems and devotional poems as well:

1 I lodge a complaint to God for what I suffer from an eye disease
    that connects my agony from dusk to dawn.
2 It is as though the puffing of my eyelids in its severity
    is an army of ants on the march in the dark of night,
3 and as if it was dust and tears mired in mud
    where pulling legs from it is a hazard.
4 It feels as though the pains in my heart come from the thrust of a needle
    between my eyeballs and my eyelids,
5 and that if there were a deep sea in my eye
    filling the borders of my two eyelids with pus,
6 then water would squirt out from it
    whenever it drops on them fire upon fire during my sleep.
7 How many a night have I spent unable to sleep
    and unable to imagine a clear bright morning.
8 My one eyelid spends the night sharing blackened blood
    with its sibling, both nourished by just the right amount.
9 In a ring of darkness you do not see any glow from the horizon
    that would appear to seeing eyes at the first shimmer of morning.

10 It is as though the light of dawn (*al-sharq*) is a merchant who was cheated
by paying for camphor* but receiving only tar.
[* Used for relieving pain and itching from inflammation.]
11 It appears as if the sun has been returned to a galaxy
motionless, not revolving around what God has created.
12 I feel as though the night is blindfolded and does not see
the silver (*dirham*) moon from which to take the gold (*dinar*).
13 My eyelid complains to the other eyelid of its illness
like one neighbor complains of an injustice to another.
14 Thanks be to God, who removes the light from darkness,
and who makes the night soothe the eyes.
15 How far were the people in judging my condition,
when my disease, by the will of God, was near a cure.
(Diwan #124: 201–202)

Ibn Hamdis's evocations and pleas to God at this time of his life, and especially in these and other devotional verses, reflect both a resignation to the human condition and a search for comfort and spiritual guidance. These late-life verses, once again, contrast sharply with his earlier political poetry in which he projects images of God, Allah, as the Divine Creator and Master of Heaven and Earth, the ultimate lawgiver who entrusts the deputies of his *umma* on earth to command right and forbid wrong. The God of his old-age, particularly in his ascetic verses, is more a loving and merciful God to whom the poet offers his supplications for comfort and forgiveness. However, being a man with a cause, and a poet who always sought out the largest audiences possible, and who took every opportunity to plead his case, Ibn Hamdis composed his late-life verses, or his poetry of old-age, fully conscious of his time and place.

By the early decades of the twelfth century, mysticism had become a widely accepted religious practice or orientation among the three faiths of the Mediterranean. In Islam, mysticism ranged from a pure ascetic devotion to membership in a growing number of social groupings. Poetry had by this time become a favorite vehicle for mystical expression. Ibn Hamdis, shuffling among Muslim, Christian, and Jewish communities through the Mediterranean, and profoundly conscious of the processes of a dynamic Arabic literary history, undoubtedly reached out to those Muslims who would warmly embrace the 'sacred' verses of an old man longing to return to his homeland. More significantly, it was an aging population of Muslim Sicilian exiles, the majority of whom relocated to their ancestral home of Ifriqiya, who would respond most fervently to his poetic messages of loss, alienation, and exile.

SICILY FOREVER ON THE MIND

All the while he was looking more inwardly, reflecting on his long life, and meditating on the life hereafter, Ibn Hamdis never abandoned his true callings: poetry and Sicily. In the year in which he died, he composed an elegy, forty-two lines long (Diwan #301: 482–485), which he dedicated, according to the introductory notice in the diwan, to Commander Abu al-Hasan ibn 'Ali Hamdun al-Sanhaji, a high-ranking officer in the Hammadid army from Bejaia, and three others to whom he refers as 'noble leaders,' one of which is explicitly named as Commander Muhammad Ma'mun. There are verses in another elegy Ibn Hamdis composed to 'Ali Ibn Hamdun (Diwan #103: 173–176) that suggest that Ibn Hamdis had made his acquaintance during his brief sojourn at Qal'at Bani Hammad, and that he later died in battle. The names of both of these men appear in historian Ibn al-Athir's account on the Hammadid attack to wrest control of Mahdia from the Zirids in the early years of the 1130s. The causes of the siege were rooted in the longstanding feud between the Hammadid and Zirid cousins. In the current atmosphere of chaos and competition for the loyalty of the numerous Arab tribes whose numbers and militias swelled to threatening levels, the Hammadid prince, Yahya ibn al-'Aziz, dispatched a militia to seize Mahdia. The sketchy details of the account, and the fact that King Roger II dispatched his own battalion to assist the Zirid al-Hasan ibn 'Ali, renders Ibn Hamdis's elegy to Ibn 'Ali Hamdun at once puzzling and understandable: any enemy of Roger II is an enemy of mine! Above all, both of the family elegies he would compose in the last year of his life bear witness to a man, not at all withdrawn, but one politically conscious and still very much committed to his cause.

ELEGY TO A NEPHEW AND FAMILY HISTORY

If it were not enough of life's hardships to suffer the loss of a homeland, to be sentenced to a life in exile, to lose a father, grandfather, aunt, and wife, to be forced to walk with a cane and bear the agony of blindness, then the loss of a nephew and a daughter soon to follow would usher in the darkest hours of Ibn Hamdis's long and painful old age. It is one thing to witness the passing of adults, but to outlive one's own children or the children of siblings stands among the most painful of human experiences, and it overloads the burden of growing old.

At the age of eighty, however, 'Abd al-Jabbar still maintained sufficient discipline, focus, and the mental and physical stamina required to compose a long 79-line elegy to the son of his sister. Lines 1–25 collapse by now familiar verses of existential despair, i.e., the cruel twists of fate and images of the life-death cycle with sentiments of personal anguish. Lines 26–31 bemoan the hardships of life in exile, and they give voice to his most candid admission of guilt he feels for not being there:

26 O nephew [son of my sister], I will remain a brother in grief
until I rest my head on the pillow of my tomb.
27 I am a man ridden with despair
for abandoning my family and moving far from my homeland.
28 The stranger (*gharib*) is afflicted with an illness that causes torment,
and this is a malady unknown (*ghariba*) to those attending to the ill.
29 I was promised a hope that threatened me with doom,
a hope in which the promise was clipped by the threat.
30 A man alive or dead, in times of disaster, may be far away,
but how different is this distance from me.
31 The announcer of your death came to me,
and even if I live on after this horror, I live against my will.

The poem is remarkable in that it draws his audience into the family history. Lines 32–51 rework images of the traditional war song, of brave and steadfast soldiers, that allow him to boast of his and the deceased nephew's forbears who came to Sicily as holy warriors and who sacrificed their lives to repel the enemy in the service of God. Lines 58–60 honor the memory of the deceased's father, Ibn Hamdis's cousin and brother-in-law, who grew up to become an accomplished physician:

58 Not even Hippocrates can stand above your father in curing
what the patient suffers from time and time again.
59 [Your father] is the more astute in his diagnoses,
and in his judgements on the causes and consequences of illnesses.
60 But could he cure a disease and thus prevent a death
after the disease has spread throughout the body?
61 By God, never! Your own death has been decreed,
from the time of birth, and by the hand of fate.

The elegy draws to a close with Ibn Hamdis calling attention to his own physical decline, defeat, and perhaps most poignantly, the fading of his poetry. He finishes the elegy by drawing a comparison between his nephew and the Prophet's son who also preceded his father in death:

71 Now in the eightieth year of my life
when chronic ailments have fastened my shackles with humiliation,
72 I drag along like a broken-footed camel,
and I fear a hostile death is about to assault me.
73 My garden of literary flowers has withered
when its full bloom once delighted those seeking delights.
74 Had you lived on after me, you would have been ransomed by others
with newly acquired or inherited wealth.
75 Be patient, O Abu al-Hasan, with the patience of one who submits to God,
in matters pertaining to the beginnings and ends of things.
76 I have watched you closely over the many events in time,
and even the most severe of them did not overburden you.

77 Was not Ibrahim, the son of Muhammad,
destined to decay and decompose after he was interred?
78 The Prophet scattered over him the dust of his gravesite
with the protective hand of prophethood.
79 So, rest in the solace in the example of the Prophet's son,
and you will follow the path of righteous guidance.
(Diwan #78: 119–124)

MOURNING A DAUGHTER, MOURNING A HOMELAND

Among the last of his poems, written a short time before his death, is an elegy to a daughter whom he refers to in line 38 as *Kifaah*, meaning in Arabic 'struggle,' an appropriate name as metaphor for the story of how Ibn Hamdis lived and defined his life. Perhaps the most telling line in the poem that binds the relationship between poet and eulogized, and father and daughter, is line 28: "I see myself as a stranger bereft of a stranger, as though we were both yearning for a homeland and family."

1 We are living our days in slumber as arrows take aim at us,
and we are nurtured and find sweetness in the bitterness of colocynth.
2 Death has dedicated itself to people when they are off guard,
and it watches vigilantly over them, morning and evening.
3 I see that life up above will totally vanish
if our world ceases to exist on this earth below.
4 There will remain a God of what existed before His creation,
One who guided with His messengers those gone astray.
5 He sends resurrection to those who are above and below the earth,
and to Him we glorify His beneficence.
6 I see the vision of death that has come alive before my eyes;
I am one of an age who should be wary of such a sight.
7 One of death's hands was about to shake my hand,
and one of its feet was about to step on mine.
8 In the ebb and tide of my breathing
exists a survival of spirit [but one] not tied to a rope.

9 Eighty years have I lived and I have found them
destroying what they built, bringing down whomever they raised.
10 Here I am living in a world speaking of hope,
and when I coveted it, I only found it dying in deed.
11 If God never granted you prosperity, you will always be deprived of it,
no matter what you do of wise and noble deeds.
12 O you who ask me about the people of my time, leave them!
For, the proof of the branches is found in the roots.
13 If you find something wrong in your own time,
then be aware of depending upon even a friend.
14 I have reflected in my full mind and feeble mind;
so say if asked: I have seen the old man in the life of a child.
15 Anguish is a heavy burden for an old man,
how I wish its weight fell on the neck of a younger one.
16 I return to recalling the inevitability of death,
with its long history of treachery and deceit.
17 How many eagles perched on the tops of the highest mountains
have perished by being devoured by flies.
18 How many lions have walked into the throes of death
and found a passage between its twisted fangs.
19 There is no watering hole in death we cannot easily swallow,
as one who comes to be quenched the first time need not a second drink.
20 My little shrub whom I planted for reward, I have moved her
to the shelter of my protection, deep within my soul.
21 I married her to a gentleman whom I praised as kind,
and she never faulted me for her life with him.
22 The news of your death came to me and rekindled the flames of my grief,
like a fire in a forest dense with trees.
23 They announced my death to you while I was still alive;
you could not blacken your eyes with kohl, since you donned the [black] robe of mourning.
24 The reports of my death were being heard throughout the lands,
as they passed from the tongue of one traveler to another.
25 You mourned a living soul whose youth was killed by Time,
what he was once endowed with will never return.

26 You died according to God's will and I did not die,
and I remain without an angel of death to record my deeds.
27 You left a spirit, and its drawing away from you
was slower than the crawling of ants on the body.
28 I see myself as a stranger bereft of a stranger,
both of us yearning for a homeland and family.
29 She cried for me thinking that I had died before her;
but I live, and she has died and is now mourned by me.
30 She performed funeral rites when my death was reported to her;
she wept as all people weep, with drizzling tears and
downpours.
31 Each person cried for me to the degree of his distress,
and each one performed what was required of him.
32 O dweller of the grave whose resting grounds
embrace your filial piety, your faith, and your virtue,
33 a mortal sadness has struck you because of my death.
Could it be that death has found you because of me?
34 You leave behind daughters in the bosom of depression,
grieving for a mother separated from her brood,
35 like the chicks of doves, targeted by the eagle from its nest
that is like the lion on the hunt.
36 May the verses of poetry cry gushes of tears for you,
like tears of white doves on the branches of tamarisk trees.
37 May every oryx hovering around your grave in the desert weep
for you,
because your eyes in all their beauty look like their eyes.
38 May their tears water a tomb for Kifaah on a moistened land,
with rain that has on fertility the same effect as drought.
39 O Lord, how many a person was there from whom I never
hoped for succor,
for weak men cannot embitter or sweeten.
40 By Your clemency, forgive the gravity of my sins.
Your generosity compensates my depravity, Your wisdom
my ignorance.

(Diwan #245: 364–367)

This elegy reveals a poet somber in his grief and philosophical in his resignation to fate, but a resignation that comes with it a strong tone of cynicism; what we build is destroyed; people do not keep to their word; and friends cannot be trusted. It also sheds light on the tragic circumstances of her death. Rumors circulated that Ibn Hamdis had himself died, and that his daughter, the mother of young children herself, was so moved to grief that she passed away soon thereafter. The fact of physical distance between father and daughter, both of whom received their information from passing travelers, binds his grief over her death to his remorse and guilt for his separation from the family. One need only recall Ibn Hamdis's qasida, mentioned earlier, in which he replied with a rejection to his cousin's pleas to rejoin the family, to understand that this separation was self-imposed. Also, the shift from third person to second person in both elegies enhances the personal anguish the poet is suffering over separation and loss. Last, the elegy to the daughter's recurring images of moist land, tamarisk trees, white doves, and other natural phenomena bring this elegy into harmony with the many poems he composed to revive the memory of his native Sicily with images, real or imagined.

DEATH AND BURIAL

The thirteenth-century historian Ibn Khallikan (1211–1282), author of a voluminous biographical dictionary, reports in his obituary on Ibn Hamdis that the poet died on the island of Majorca off the coast of Spain in the month of Ramadan, 527 AH (June, 1133 AD), and that he was buried in a tomb next to that of Ibn al-Labbana, the famous Andalusian poet who served along with Ibn Hamdis as court poet to al-Muʿtamid in Seville. Ibn al-Athir adds that historians differ on the place of burial, some saying that Ibn Hamdis was buried in Bejaia, on the northeast coast of Algeria. While both are within the realm of possibility, it would be hard to imagine that a blind and infirm octogenarian, recently bereaved of loved ones and still following closely the events of his beloved homeland close by, would board a ship and embark on such a journey at this late stage of his life. Ibn Khallikan also inserts a quotation from Ibn Bassam, Andalusian philologist and literary historian who was a contemporary of Ibn Hamdis:

> [Ibn Hamdis was] a highly skilled poet who coined innovative meanings with precision, and who expressed them with precious and elegant

words. He practiced versatility in striking just the right metaphors, and he immersed himself in the vast ocean of lexicography to extract the pearl of the most hidden meaning.

(Ibn Khallikan III: 212)

These two reports that have survived in Ibn Khallikan's obituary of Ibn Hamdis shed light on how the poet was viewed in the years that followed his death: first, that he was master craftsmen of words who had a powerful and creative poetic sensibility; and that he was well known for his association with Muslim Spain. The idea that he would be buried next to Ibn al-Labbana in faraway Majorca may very well be a figment of Ibn Bassam's Andalusian fantasy. Given the extraordinary preponderance of his homeland as a recurring theme in his poetry, which many anthologists do in fact mention, it is clear that Ibn Hamdis was and remains today unequivocally associated with Sicily and would have preferred to be remembered as such. However, in light of the massive impact of eight centuries of Arab Islamic civilization in medieval Spain, and under the weight of its formidable textual archive, it would seem logical that Ibn Hamdis earned a place in Andalusian literary history, as much for his years in Seville as for the artistic affinities his poetry shared with that of his Spanish colleagues.

This was not, however, the way 'Abd al-Jabbar Ibn Hamdis viewed his world. In his eyes the island of Sicily, the place of his birth and the center of his universe, was a sparkling jewel in the crown of Islam, the hard-earned prize won after years of conquest to bring faith and knowledge onto the shores of infidelity. Alongside the proverbial Hima and the imagined abodes of Darin, Abraq, and Hims, Sicily became home to the noble Arabs who for centuries were celebrated for their *hasab wa nasab*, their nobility and sum total of noble qualities. Throughout his entire life, he kept a watchful eye over it, hopefully and hopelessly, and he dedicated his poetry to pleading its return to *Dar al-Islam*.

IBN HAMDIS'S LEGACY IN HISTORY AND LITERATURE

'Abd al-Jabbar Ibn Hamdis lived in time we designate today as the *medieval world*, or the *Middle Ages*, but his life and his poetry share affinities with those of a modern man. It should also be noted that he was a citizen of the Mediterranean world. His was a time and place that experienced at once a complex of cross-cultural conflict and coexistence among peoples of different faiths and cultures. The many *bloody* battles for political and economic dominance, as well as contentious religious and cultural rivalries tallied with incidents of sharing a common life. The last three decades of Ibn Hamdis's life coincided with the early stages of what historians have labeled as the 'Twelfth Century Renaissance' in which Arabic learning, especially in philosophy and the sciences, reached Latin Christendom via a robust translation movement in which Sicily and the royal patronage of Roger II played a key role.

Ibn Hamdis was first and foremost a committed writer (*engagé* or *multazim*), utterly and completely devoted to his art in the service of his community. He learned his craft by immersing himself in the study of centuries of Arabic philology in all its branches. His poetry was at once imbued with a highly intricate and studious intertextuality with his revered predecessors and with a bold and creative lexical and rhetorical inventiveness. It was his literary genius to put his relentless devotion to reading and rereading the Arabic poetic canons in communion with the events and anxieties of his times, of displacement, expulsion and exile. Poetry for Ibn Hamdis was the weapon to fight what he saw as all the wrongs and injustices in his world. The result was that he drew from his personal experiences of loss, betrayal, and estrangement to create a vast poetic volume of poetry endowed with a unique voice to tell the [hi]story of Muslim Sicily.

Ibn Hamdis was a pan-Arabist, long before the coining of the term in the early twentieth century. His world view was centered on a 'nation' of people who shared a common language and history. His poetry maps the diversity of the Arabian landscape that stretched from the Red Sea to the Indian Ocean, crossing over to Mesopotamia and the Levant, cutting through Egypt and extending across the North African littoral that came to include Spain and Sicily. His verses are a celebration of the multiplicity of Arabian tribes in all their mythical and historical heroics and codes of honor, evoking events, places, and names that came to define Arab history and identity.

Third, Ibn Hamdis was a pan-Muslim. He lived in a time and place where a strict sacred/profane divide did not exist, and he saw himself as a 'citizen' of the Islamic *umma* ruled by sacred law and civilized by a worldly humanism. He saw no contradiction in his poems that began with verses celebrating a night of bibulous revelry and ending with praise or a plea to God. As a consummate poet steeped in the classical tradition, he injected his poems with evocations of the *jahili* behemoth of Fate in all its cruelty and deception; and as a devout believer, he expanded the poem with verses describing God's justice and mercy that ultimately triumph over humanity. Ibn Hamdis's poetry, especially in his panegyrics and battle verses, drew heavily from the Prophet Muhammad's struggles with both pagan practices and political foes as examples of true faith and valor. His verses aimed to unify his audiences and to inspire his brethren in joining forces to defend the faith and repel the enemies of God. Living in a time of a surging Christian conquest, Ibn Hamdis's poetry drew on the rhetoric of jihad as a weapon against crusade, but also a jihad of self-sacrifice that promoted a very specific Muslim morality. He wove into his poetry citations, allusions, and references from the Quran, hadith, and other scriptural writings to convey messages of justice and righteousness that aimed to inspire his readers and audiences.

Last, Ibn Hamdis was a Sicilian nationalist, long before the rise of the modern nation-state and the ideology of nationalism. Rare it is to find in the Arabic literary *heritage*, a term coined in the nineteenth century by reformist intellectuals in the Arab world as *al-turath*, i.e., the sum total of Arabic Islamic writing produced in pre-modern history, an individual who would identify himself to one land to the extent and degree that 'Abd al-Jabbar Ibn Hamdis clung to Sicily. In the medieval Muslim world, a man or woman would self-identify or be identified through genealogy, religion, place of origin, or the place where one practiced a profession or trade, or where one achieved fame for outstanding accomplishments.

In the course of his professional life and the poetry he crafted, Ibn Hamdis mapped Sicily onto the grand civilization of *Dar al-Islam*, especially as it extended throughout the Mediterranean Basin of the Middle Ages. He imagined and extolled his homeland as a frontier of Islam, the living proof of the unexpected but near-miraculous achievement of the Islamic conquest to expand the boundaries of the true faith, knowledge, and civilization. His life journey began in Syracuse and progressed to Sfax, Seville, Marrakesh, Majorca, Bejaia, and Mahdia. And at each and every encampment he alighted, he unpacked his saddlebag filled with his memories of Sicily and his resolve to return there one day.

Ibn Hamdis joined Sicily to a monumental Arabic *republic of letters*. The quality and quantity of his poetry, in all its exquisite philological texture and its precise historical worldliness, assured Sicily an eternal place in the vast library of Arabic literature. By way of his dedication to his art and his loyalty to his homeland (*watan*), Sicily as the poetic beloved, the abandonment encampment, the paradise lost, and the object of memory somehow made its way, textually, contextually, or sub-textually, into the panegyrics, elegies, love poems, wine songs, battle scene segments, and devotional pieces he composed.

Ibn Hamdis the Sicilian, by way of his unwavering loyalty and life-long identification with the land of his birth, adds a powerful, if not unique, individual voice to Muslim Sicily. His voluminous anthology of poetry, a literary tour-de-force that bears testament to love and devotion to a homeland, situates *Siqilliya* along a continuum of world civilizations that came to define Sicily. It was especially through a keen historical perspective he infused into his oeuvre, combined with his undivided attention to the twists and turns unfolding in his own time, that he succeeds in marking Muslim Sicily's place in world history. His lifelong project was to celebrate, document, recall, and remind his audiences and readers of Arabic and Islam's chapter in Sicily's rich history that boasts Phoenician, Greek, Roman, Byzantine, and later Norman periods. Coming between the Byzantine and the Norman eras, Arab-Muslim civilization added richly to the historical progression and cultural development of the island. Although he was fated never to return, he found his way home, back to Muslim Sicily, through his writing. His diwan in all its literary artistry and historical detail expresses that better than any other individual.

In drawing to a close, I give the poet the last word:

1 In times of great stress we urge on our camels,
and their feet carry us through the vast wastelands,

2 frightening the wide-eyed wild cows to scatter in the desert,
cows whose eyes reminds us of lovely young maidens.
3 Virgins, you see their exceptionally rare beauty
in harmony with and exemplar of their own species.
4 O reproacher, let me unleash my tears, for in my utmost patience,
I have found nothing to stop their flow.
5 I am a man who has resigned to a sorrow
that has left a scar in my heart.
6 I always thought that my homeland would return to its people,
but such thinking was wrong, and I am now in despair.
7 I consoled my soul when I saw it
suffering an unfortunate, fatal disease.
8 How can it be that it was forced to endure humiliation,
when its mosques in the hands of Christians have now become churches?
9 Whenever the monks wish to strike, they do so
by sounding the bells, night and day.
10 If every medicine fails at making a cure,
then how can the polisher remove the rust from the sword?
11 Ah, Sicily! Time has violated its lands,
where it once was the beacon for people of all time.
12 Many a fearful eye had kept vigil throughout the night,
but then relaxed their guard out of feeling safe and secure.
13 I see my country humiliated by the Christians,
while the glory of my people still stands strong.
14 The lands of the infidel once donned the garments of fear,
but now it is in my homeland these robes they wear.
15 I miss seeing the Arab lions [strutting] amongst their ranks,
in whose paws you would see these barbarians as prey.
16 But my eye has not seen such as those in battle,
whose spears strike the strike of war heroes.
17 How often the flash of a pointed sword you imagined in the thick of battle,
like the twinkling of stars on a dark night.
18 They secretly insert themselves amidst the tips of the lances,
to smite the knights off their saddles.
19 I never imagined that the heat of fire would turn cold
as it hit the dried branches of palm trees in the heat of day.

20 Calabria was subject to their many raids,
when Arabs annihilated their fiercest commanders and knights.
21 They opened the bolted gates of its city with their swords,
and left it with its lights extinguished.
22 They took as prisoners many fair-haired maidens unveiled,
whose long hair you would take as their hoods.
23 The Arabs would cross the deep sea to reach them,
in vast numbers, like a sea whose waves are warriors,
24 in a warship launched by its burning fuel,
with the stench of death overwhelming the senses.
25 You see them as though covered in red and yellow felt,
like daughters of dark-skinned men (*zanj*) being paraded as brides.
26 When the brick ovens fill up with smoke,
you would imagine them as erupting volcanoes.
27 Is there in Castrogiovanni a patch of land still to be inhabited,
while many a trace of Islam has been obliterated?
28 Is it any wonder that these demons have knocked down
the galaxies of stars, and turned them into places to sit?
29 Syracuse had become for them a land of last resistance,
where they now visit sepulchres in the two monasteries.
30 They trampled on a land whose people are below the earth,
and where there [now] remains no one to resist them.
31 If these graves were to break open,
then emerging from them would be the fiercest of lions.
32 But I have seen in the forest that when the lion is away,
the wolf struts about on his turf.

(Diwan #157: 274–276)

BIBLIOGRAPHY

‘Abbas, Ihsan (1994). *Mu‘jam al-‘Ulama’ wa al-Shu‘ara’ al-Siqilliyin*. Beirut: Dar al-gharb al-islami.

—— (1960). *Al-‘Arab fi Siqilliya*. Cairo: Dar al-Ma‘arif.

Abun-Nasr, Jamil M. (1987). *A History of the Maghrib in the Islamic Period*. Cambridge: Cambridge University Press.

Amari, Michele (1933). *Storia dei Musulmani di Sicilia* (edited by C.A. Nallino). Catania.

—— (1857). *Biblioteca Arabo-Sicula*. Lipsia: F.A. Brockhaus.

Bouyahya, Chedly (1972). *La Vie Littéraire en Ifriqiya sous les Zirides*. Tunis: S.T.D.

Brett, Michael (2010). "The Central Lands of North Africa and Sicily, Until the Beginning of the Almohad Period." *The New Cambridge History of Islam* (edited by Michael Cook et. al.). Volume II: 46–64.

Catlos, Brian (2018). *Kingdoms of Faith: A New History of Islamic Spain*. New York: Basic Books.

de Cenival, Pierre (1932). "Le Prétendue Evêché de la Kal‘a des Beni Hammad." *Hespéris*: XV: 1–10.

Gabrieli, Francesco (1954). "Arabi di Sicilia e Arabi di Spagna." *Dal Mondo dell'Islam*. Naples: Riccardo Ricciardi: 88–108.

Gil, Moshe. (1995). "Sicily 827–1072, in light of the Geniza documents and parallel sources." *Italia Judaica* V: 96–171.

Granara, William (2019). *Narrating Muslim Sicily: War and Peace in the Medieval Mediterranean World*. London: I.B. Tauris.

—— (2018). "The Battle of Zallaqa Between *Mythos* and *Logos*," in *Convivencia and Medieval Spain: Essays in Honor of Thomas F. Glick* (edited by Mark T. Abate). Palgrave MacMillan: 253–275.

—— (2013). "Sicilian Poets in Seville: Literary Affinities across Political Boundaries," in *A Sea of Languages: Rethinking the Arabic Role in Medieval Literary History* (edited by K. Mallette and S. C. Akbari). Toronto: University of Toronto Press: 199–216.

—— (2012). "Ibn Ḥamdis's al-Dīmās Qaṣīda: Memorial to a Fallen Homeland," in *The Value of Poetry in Reconstructing Arab History* (edited by Ramzi Baalbaki, Saleh Said Agha, and Tarif Khalidi). Beirut: American University of Beirut Press: 247–262.

—— (2011). "Ibn Hamdis," in *Essays in Arabic Literary Biography 925–1350* (edited by Terri DeYoung and Mary St. Germain). Wiesbaden: Harrassowitz Verlag; 145–150.

—— (2008). "Rethinking Muslim Sicily's Golden Age: Poetry and Patronage at the Fatimid Court," in *I Fatimidi e il Mediterraneo*. Palermo: *Alifba*: 95–108.

—— (1998). "Remaking Muslim Sicily: Ibn Hamdis & the Poetics of Exile," in *Edebiyat* 9:168–198.

Al-Himyari, Muhammad Abu 'Abdallah (1937). *Kitab al-Rawd al-Mi'tar fi Khabar al-Aqtar* (edited by É. Lévi-Provençal). Cairo: Matba'at al-ta'lif wa al-tarjama wa al-nasr.

Ibn Hamdis, 'Abd al-Jabbar (1960). *Diwan* (edited by Ihsan 'Abbas). Cairo: Dar al- Ma'arif.

Ibn Jubayr, Muhammad ibn Ahmad (1952). *The Travels of Ibn Jubayr* (translated with introduction and notes by R. J. C. Broadhurst). London: J. Cape.

Ibn Khallikan, Shams al-Din Abu al-'Abbas (1977). *Wafayat al-a'yan wa anba' al-zaman* (edited by Ihsan 'Abbas). Beirut: Dar Sadir.

Johns, Jeremy (2002). *Arabic Administration in Norman Sicily*. Cambridge, UK: Cambridge University Press.

King, Matthew (2018). *The Norman Kingdom of Africa and the Medieval Mediterranean*. Ph.D. Thesis: University of Minnesota.

Metcalfe, Alex (2009). *The Muslims of Medieval Sicily*. Edinburgh University Press.

Monroe, James (1974). *Hispano-Arabic Poetry*. Berkeley: University of California Press.

Ruggles, D. Fairchild (1994). "Vision and Power at the Qala Bani Hammad in Islamic North Africa." *Journal of Garden History*: 28–41.

INDEX

'Abbad II al'Mu'tadid bi-allah 49
'Abbadids 48–9, 50–1, 53–4, 80–4
'Abbasids 6–7, 15, 22, 36, 37, 88
'Abd al-'Aziz al-Siqilli 116
'Abd al-Ghani 115
'Abd al-Jabbar, *see* Ibn Hamdis
'Abd al-Rahman ibn Muhammad ibn 'Umar al-Buthayri 131
'Abd al-Rahman III, Emir 51
abstinence 126
abstract noun (*zuhd*) 126
Abu al-'Arab 53
Abu al-Daw' Siraj ibn Ahmad ibn Raja' 131–2
Abu al-Hasan 'Ali Hamdun al-Sanhaji 138
Abu al-Hasan 'Ali ibn Yusuf Ibn Abi al-Dar (cousin/brother-in-law) 105, 107–9
Abu al-Qasim Muhammad ibn 'Abbad 49
Abu Bakr (father) 6, 26–7
Abu Bakr (son) 106–7
Abu Hafs 'Umar ibn Hasan 131
Abu Hanifa 21, 22
Abu Muhriz 21, 22
Abu Yazid Mulkhallad ibn Kayrad 35
active participle (*zaahid*) 126
adab (belles-lettres) 11
Adelaide de Vasto, Countess of Sicily 130
Aghlabids 2, 23; *see also* Ziyadat-Allah I, Emir
Aghmat 80, 86
agriculture 37, 69, 102
al-Akhal, Ahmad ibn Yusuf 4, 5
Aledo 70–1
Aleppo 51
Alfonso VI of León and Castile, King 49, 61, 69, 70–1, 73, 74–80
Algeria, *see* Bejaia
'Ali ibn Hamdun 138
'Ali ibn Yahya 35, 112, 116, 118–19, 120, 121
'Ali ibn Yusuf ibn Tashufin 120–1
Almohads 34, 123–4
Almoravids xiii, 34, 72, 73–4, 102
  and Almohads 123–4
  and Zirids 120–3
Amari, Michele 26, 27
amatory preface (*nasib*) xiv, 30, 38, 63
al-Andalus 11, 12, 15, 145
  and Almoravids 120–1
  and battles 70–2
  and Christians 69
  and Ibn Hamdis 145
  and al-Zallaqa 72–80
  see also Cordoba; Seville

animals 16–17, 30–1, 45, 90
Apulia 4, 101, 102
Arabic language 10, 13, 20
Arabs 37–45, 146
Asad ibn al-Furat 6–7, 21–3
asceticism 126
Azdi tribe 6
al-ʻAziz 3

Badis ibn al-Mansur ibn Buluggin 87
Badis ibn Mansur 36
Baghdad 6, 11, 22, 25, 36, 37
  and Buyid Court 51
  and al-Muʻizz ibn Badis 95
Banu Hilal tribe 33, 37, 39, 44, 95
Banu Sulaym tribe 33, 37, 39, 95
Banu Kalb, *see* Kalbids
Banu Lakhm tribe 48
Banu Ziri tribe 87
al-Barghawati, Hamu ibn Malil 34
al-Barghawati, Mansur 34
battle scenes 63, 89, 97, 121–3, 148
Bedouins 39, 40, 44
Bejaia 86–94, 144
Berbers xiii, 3, 4–5, 23, 33
  and al-Andalus 49, 70–1
  see also Almohads; Almoravids; Zirids
al-Bilanubi, Abu al-Hasan ʻAli 7
blindness 136–8
boast (*fakhr*) 38
Borsa, Roger, *see* Roger I, Count of Sicily
bravery (*shajaʻa*) 38, 40, 57, 71, 89, 97–100
Buluggin ibn Ziri 87
Buyids 51
Byzantines 3, 6, 9, 20–1, 23, 101

Cairo 25, 35, 52
Calabria 4, 102, 121
caliphate 2–3, 6, 23, 35–7
  and Cordoba 48–9, 51, 54
Castrogiovanni 1, 2, 85, 101
Catania 1, 2
Catlos, Brian 70
chameleons 30–1
Christianity 3, 4, 9, 15, 25–6
  and Arabic learning 146
  and crucifix (*salib*) 31, 32
  and Ibn Hamdis 16
  and Italian mainland 133
  and Qalʻat Bani Hammad 88–9
  see also Alfonso VI of León and Castile, King; crusades
Constantine X Ducas, Emperor 101
Cordoba 25, 48, 49, 51, 73, 90
  and fall 61–2
cosmology 16
courage, *see* bravery
court poetry 48, 51–2, 60–1, 62, 112–13
crusades 74, 102, 147
culture 11–12, 13–14

Damascus 25
Day of Judgement 82, 111, 127
death–life cycle 30
departure (*rahil*) 38, 45, 90
description (*wasf*) 16, 17, 90
desert 16, 30, 38–9, 40–5, 90
determination (*ʻazm*) 31–2, 38
devotional verse (*zuhdiyya*) 125–8, 148
al-Dimas, battle of 121–3, 125, 128
diwan xiv, 7–8, 9, 14–17
  #27: 96–100
  #28: 105–6
  #29: 27–32
  #30: 126–7
  #33: 114–15
  #71: 61

#78: 139–41
#101: 57–60
#103: 138
#110: 18
#120: 71–2
#124: 136–7
#132: 115
#133: 116–17
#134: 117
#138: 119
#143: 122–3
#152: 81
#157: 148–50
#166: 111
#172: 17
#199: 14
#227: 113–14
#245: 141–4
#269: 40–5
#270: 103–4
#282: 108
#283: 75–80
#297: 106–7
#300: 135
#301: 138
#325: 85–6
#330: 55–7
#335: 82–4
#344: 48
#349: 90–4

Egypt 3, 4, 5, 12, 16; *see also* Cairo; Fatimids
elegies (*ritha'*) 54–7, 82–4, 148
and family 105–9, 139–44
and Roger II 132
and Zirids 116–17
elites 8, 13, 23, 33, 36, 48, 107
Elvira of Castille 130
emigration 52, 96
eulogies, *see* elegies
Euphemius 20–1
exile 30, 128

Fate 26, 38, 105–6, 108, 147
and devotional verse 125, 128
Fatimids 2–3, 5, 23–4, 52
and Hammadids 88
and Sicily 101
and Zirids 35, 36, 112, 120
Fernando of Castile, Count 74
al-Fihri, al-Sharif ʻAli ibn Ahmad 115, 116, 117
forbearance (*hilm*) 38
France 37

Gabes 118–19, 121
Gabriele, Francesco 54
genealogy (*nasab*) 39
generosity (*jud/karam*) 38, 40, 57, 89
Genoa 95, 119
genres 7–8; *see also* devotional verse; elegies; love songs; odes; panegyrics; war songs; wine songs
George of Antioch 35, 119, 124
Germany 102
gnomic introduction (*muqaddima hikamiyya*) 29–30, 117
Gregory VII, Pope 88
Guiscard, Robert, Duke of Apulia 26, 101, 102

hadith 9, 10, 147
Hamdanids 51
Hammad ibn Buluggin 87
Hammadids 36, 87–94, 112, 120, 138
Hanafis 21–2, 23–4
al-Hasan ibn ʻAli 20, 35, 122, 123, 124, 125, 138
Hebrew 16

al-Himyari, Muhammad:
Kitab al-Rawd al-Mi'tar (Book of the Perfumed Garden) 73, 74–5, 78
holy war, *see* jihad
honorableness (*hasab wa nasab*) 38, 40
hospitality (*ijara wa diyafa*) 38, 57, 60
humor 17

Ibn 'Abbad (Benavert) 102–3
Ibn 'Ammar 49, 60–1
Ibn Anas 21
Ibn al-Athir 96, 129, 138, 144
Ibn 'Atiq, Abu Said 'Uthman 52
Ibn Bassam 144–5
Ibn al-Birr, Abu Bakr 11, 12
Ibn al-Fahham, 'Abd al-Rahman 12
Ibn Hamdis, Abu Muhammad 'Abd al-Jabbar xiii–xiv, 6, 7–8, 11
and age 111, 135–8
and Almoravids 120–1
and Arabs 37–45
and battles 71–2
and blindness 136–8
and death 144–5
and departure 27–32
and devotional verse 125–8
and al-Dimas 121–3
and education 8–9
and family 26–7, 105–9, 139–44
and father 54–7
and Gabes 118–19
and homeland 17–18
and al-Idrisi 133
and Jawhara 85–6
and legacy 145–50
and Mahdia 94–5
and al-Mu'tamid ibn 'Abbad 63–7, 80–4
and Normans 101
and panegyrics 57–60
and Qal'at Bani Hammad 87–94
and Roger II 130
and Seville 47–8, 50–1, 54, 60–1, 62–3
and Sfax 19–20, 33, 34
and Sicilian commanders 115–16, 138–9
and Sicily 103–4
and Tamim ibn al-Mu'izz 95–100
and Yahya ibn Tamim 112–15, 116–18
and al-Zallaqa 75–80
and Zirids 35–6, 124
see also diwan
Ibn Hawqal, Abu al-Qasim ibn 'Ali 24–6
Ibn al-Hawwas 1–2
Ibn Jubayr, Abu al-Husayn Muhammad 50
Ibn Khaldun 37, 39
Ibn Khallikan 144–5
Ibn al-Labbana 53–4, 144
Ibn Makki, 'Umar ibn Khalaf
Tathqif al-lisan fi Talqih al-Janan 11–12
Ibn Mankut, 'Abdallah 1
Ibn al-Qatta', 'Ali ibn Ja'far 12
Ibn Rashiq, Abu 'Ali Hasan
Kitab al-'Umda 11
Ibn Tashufin, Yusuf 72, 73–4, 79, 80
Ibn al-Thumna 1–2, 101
Ibn Tumart, Abu 'Abd Allah Muhammad 123–4
Ibn Yasin, 'Abdallah 72
Ibn Zaydun, Abu Bakr 73
identity 39
al-Idrisi, Abu 'Abdallah Muhammad
Book of Roger 7, 133–4
al-Idrisi, Muhammad ibn Muhammad ibn
Kitab Nuzhat al-Mushtaq fi ikhtiraq al-Afaq (The Excursion of One

Longing to Cross the Horizons) 133–4
Ifriqiya 2, 6, 12, 30, 37–40
and jihad 9, 10, 22–4
and Zirids 35–7
see also Mahdia; Qal'at Bani Hammad; Sfax
infidels 44, 113
insects 17
introductory epigrams 48
Islam 3–6
and al-Andalus 48–9, 50–1, 61–2, 69, 70–1
and devotional verse 126, 127–8
and frontier 15
and Ibn Hamdis 16, 147–8
and Ibn Hawqal 25
and mysticism 137
and Palermo 102
and Roger II 130–3
and scholars 9–10
and Sicilian culture 11–12, 129, 145
and Yahya ibn Tamim 113, 114
see also jihad; Shi'i Islam; Sufism; Sunni Islam
Islamic law 11, 21–2
Italian mainland, *see* Apulia; Calabria; Genoa; Pisa

al-Jabbar, Abu al-Hasan 'Ali ibn 'Abd 52
Ja'far 3, 4
jahili, *see* pre-Islamic poetry
al-Jahiz 38
Jawhara 85–6
Jazirat al-Ahasi 121
jihad 3, 4, 6, 9–10, 20–1, 22–4
and Ibn Hamdis 71, 147
and Ibn Hawqal 25–6
and poetry 62
and al-Zallaqa 72–80
Johns, Jeremy 132
jurisprudence 10; *see also* Islamic law
jurists (*fuqaha'*) 21–2
justice (*'adl*) 38

Kairouan 21–2, 25, 37
Kalbids xiii, 1, 2–3, 12–13, 51–2
Kharijites 33, 34
Khaybar, Battle of 116

law, *see* Islamic law
literacy 12–13
Lombards 133
love songs (*ghazal*) 63, 148

Mahdia 5, 88, 95–100, 112–15
and Ibn Hamdis 94–5
and Normans 124
and siege 138
Majorca 144, 145
male bonding 13–14
Malikis 10, 21–2, 23–4
manliness (*muru'a*) 38
al-Mansur ibn al-Nasir ibn 'Alnas 87–8, 89, 90, 94
al-Marakushi 124
Marrakesh 72, 80
Mazara 1, 19, 22–3
Mecca 16, 128
medial segment (*gharad*) 38
Mediterranean Sea 36, 72, 112, 119–20
Mesopotamia 10, 16
metaphor 90
Morocco, *see* Aghmat, Marrakesh
mortality 125, 127
Muhammad, Prophet 16, 116, 147
Muhammad ibn 'Abbad al-Mu'tamid bi-allah 48–9
Muhammad Ma'mun 138
Muhib ibn 'Abd al-Hakam al-Siqilli 115

al-Mu'izz ibn Badis 5, 11, 34, 35, 36–7, 52
and changes 94–5
al-Mu'izz li-din Allah 35, 87
mujahidun 5, 6, 10, 23
Muslims, *see* Islam
al-Mustansir bi-allah 95
al-Mu'tamid ibn 'Abbad of Seville, King xiii, 47–8, 49, 50–1, 53, 57–61, 63–7
and Alfonso IV 70
and Ibn Hamdis 80–4, 86
and al-Zallaqa 73, 74–80
Mu'tazilism 22
muwashshah (strophic verse) 53
mysticism 137–8

al-Nasir ibn 'Alnas 87, 88–9
nationalism x, 147
nature 16
naval forces 52, 94, 112, 119–20
Nicholas II, Pope 101
Nictotera 121
noble breeding (*hasab wa nasab*) 38, 40
nomadics (*badu*) 39
Normans xiii, 2, 9, 26, 100–3
and Ifriqiya 35, 95–6
and naval dominance 112
and Palermo 129–34
and Tunisia 40
see also Roger II
North Africa 16, 118; *see also* Ifriqiya
North Africans 4–5, 10
Noto xiii, 6, 17, 39, 79
and conquest 85, 103

odes (*qasida*) 30, 37, 38, 40–5
and age 111
and 'Ali ibn Yahya 121–2
and devotional verse 125
and Ibn Hamdis 71–2, 75–80, 80–4, 81, 82–4
and *wasf* 89–90
and Yahya ibn Tamim 113
and Zirids 116
old age 111, 127, 135
Orientalism 39

Palermo xiii, 1, 2, 5, 10
and Ibn Hawqal 24–5
and Kalbid Court 51
and Normans 102, 129–34
and Roger I 17
and Zirids 112
pan-Arabism 39, 62, 146
panegyrics 7–8, 13, 35, 40–5, 148
and Abu al-'Arab 53
and Hammadids 89
and Ibn Hamdis 62, 63–7
and politics 57–60
and Roger II 130–3
and Tamim ibn al-Mu'izz 96–100
and Yahya ibn Tamim 113–15
parias (protection tax) 70
patronage 48, 112, 129
permanence 30
petty kings 48–9, 69, 70, 88
philology 10, 15
physical attributes 57
Pisa 95, 119
poetry 11–18; *see also* court poetry; diwan; genres
praise 97–100, 114, 116–17, 122–3
pre-Islamic poetry (*jahili*) 11, 15, 16, 147
and Ibn Hamdis 37, 38
see also panegyrics
present tense 97–100
protection (*ijara wa diyafa*) 38, 40, 57, 60

Qal'at Bani Hammad 87–94
qasida, *see* odes
Quran 9, 10, 147

Rafi' ibn Makan 118–19, 121
rahil, *see* departure
refugees 52, 96
renunciation 126
repentance (*tawba*) 126
rhetorical embellishment (*badi'*) 11, 13, 15, 60
rhetorical prayer (*du'a'*) 40
Roger I, Count of Sicily xiii, 17, 26, 100–1, 129
Roger II of Sicily, King 40, 118–19, 121, 129–30, 138
  and al-Idrisi 133–4
  and poetry 130–3
Ruggles, D. Fairchild 90–1

safe haven (*ijara wa idafa*) 114
Sassanians 16
sedentary (*hadar*) 39
sermon (*wa'z*) 126
Seville xiii, 45, 47–9, 50–1, 52–4, 60–7
  and 'Abbadids fall 80–4
Sfax xiii, 18, 19–20, 33, 34
  and departure 45
  and family 105–9
Shi'i Islam 23–4, 33
Sicily xiv, 6–7, 96, 100–3
  and commanders 115–16
  and Ibn Hamdis 15, 30, 103–4, 128, 138–9, 145, 147–50
  and Ifriqiya 19, 20, 22–4, 36
  and Islam 3–6, 9, 11–12
  and Spain 50–4
  see also Palermo; Roger II; Syracuse
al-Simsam, Hasan 5–6
al-Siqilli, Jawhar 35
slave corps (*'abid*) 23
Sousse 6, 19, 33, 95
Spain, *see* al-Andalus; Majorca
steadfastness 40
Sufism 11, 127
Sunni Islam 10, 20, 23–4, 33, 95
  and Almoravids 72, 121
  and Hammadids 88
  and Zirids 36–7
Syracuse xiii, 1, 6, 17, 85, 102–3
Syria 6, 10, 16, 25

Tamim ibn al-Mu'izz 95–100, 112
al-Tarabanshi, Sulayman ibn Muhammad 52
taxation 70
temporality 30
Toledo 62, 69
trade 10, 69, 72, 101–2
transformation 30
al-Tunbudhi, Mansur 22
Tunisia xiii
Twelfth Century Renaissance 146

ugly into beauty (*tajmil al-qabih*) 71
'ulama' 9, 33, 36–7
'Umar (son) 34, 106–7
Umayyads 2, 15, 51, 54
Umm Ibrahim 1–2
Urban II, Pope 74

war songs 116–17, 140
wars of conquest 16
wine songs (*khamiriyya*) 14, 63, 75, 114, 131, 148

Yahya ibn al-'Aziz 138
Yahya ibn Tamim 35, 112–18
Yemenis 16

Yusuf ibn 'Abdallah al-Kalbi,
Abu al-Futuh 3, 4

al-Zallaqa, battle of 70–1, 72–80
Zanata 35, 87, 123
Zirids xiii, 5, 9, 33, 95–100, 112–18
and Hammadids 94, 138
and Ifriqiya 35–7
and Sicily 101
see also 'Ali ibn Yahya
Ziyadat-Allah I, Emir 6, 7, 9, 16,
20–1, 22
Zoroastrianism 16
zuhdiyya, *see* devotional verse